PAULO FREIRE:
HIS LIFE, WORKS AND THOUGHT

Paulo Freire:
His Life, Works and Thought

by
Denis E. Collins, S.J.

PAULIST PRESS
New York/Ramsey/Toronto

Library of Congress
Catalog Card Number: 77-83567

ISBN: 0-8091-2056-9

Cover by Morris Berman

Cover Photo Cortesy of the
World Council of Churches

Published by Paulist Press
Editorial Office: 1865 Broadway, New York, N.Y. 10023
Business Office: 545 Island Road, Ramsey, N.J. 07446

Printed and bound in the
United States of America

Contents

For my parents

For my parents

Foreword

I owe a debt to many persons here in the United States and in Mexico who kindly gave me assistance in preparing this book. My sincere thanks to: Paulo Freire, who patiently answered my questions, to Professors Robert Brackenbury and William O'Neill of the School of Education of the University of Southern California, to Dr. Albert Jonsen of the University of California at San Francisco, to the Jesuit Community of the University of San Francisco, to Dr. Harriet Sherwin of San Francisco State University, to Rev. John Killeen, S.J., of Loyola Marymount University, to Dr. Pablo Latapi and his staff of the Centro de Estudios Educativos in Mexico City, to Señora Carmen Maza, also of Mexico City, and to Professor John Ohliger and Ms. Anne Hartung for their generous help at The Ohio State University.

I also want to say a word of special thanks to Rev. Robert J. Starratt, S.J., who introduced me to the ideas of Paulo Freire, and to all the other Jesuits too numerous to list here who helped and supported my research.

Part I
Life and Works

I

How is one to account for the optimism of Paulo Freire? Any effort such as this little book's introduction to his thought must recognize at the outset that the many adjectives—radical, utopian, aimiable, Christian, critical—which correctly describe Freire all derive from his underlying optimistic attitude about human beings. He passionately believes that all men and women can someday become as fully human and free as their Creator intends them to be.

Freire's life and work as an educator is optimistic in spite of poverty, imprisonment, and exile. He is a world leader in the struggle for the liberation of the poorest of the poor: the marginalized classes who constitute the "cultures of silence" in many lands. On a planet where more than half the people go hungry every day because nations are incapable of feeding all their citizens, where we cannot yet agree that every human being has a right to eat, Paulo Freire toils to help men and women overcome their sense of powerlessness to act in their own behalf.

What is singular about Paulo Freire is not so much the controversy sparked in debates about his revolutionary pedagogy, but the development of his educational ideas from every stage of his life and each job he has undertaken. Consonant with his premise (shared by Marx and Hegel) that reflection and action must never be undertaken independently, Freire's thought evolved from his early family life and education, and from his reflections upon those experiences and the experiences of those with whom he worked and lived. Where the development of his thought will lead him in the future is unknown, even somewhat disconcerting to his colleagues,[1] but at this time I hope that a brief sketch of Freire's life and thought will facilitate wider understanding and appreciation of his critique of traditional education and some of the attitudes and tactics he believes essential to authentic humanistic education.

If Freire is an optimist, his optimism does not stem from a-historical idealism. His writings and teaching rigorously insist that men and women educate themselves by struggling to become free in an historical mode of being and in no other. The challenges he throws down to modern educators are the agonies of millions of people who starve, who are systematically excluded from employment, who are ill-housed, whose economies are exploited by richer nations, who have no say in determining the present or future. The questions he raises are uncomfortable for us Americans, so frequently indignant at the "arrogance" of the third world. At the same time his questions are most likely the same ones that crossed the mind of Lazarus as he languished in pain at Dives' door. I am in no position to recommend one or another form of socialism as a panacea for the world's ills, but I would be less than human if I did not listen seriously to socialist critics like Freire who seek a freer society. Freire is fond of saying that he and his thought are incomplete, that he is "not yet a Christian." I submit that this is true of each of us, and that if we could but remember it, dialogue with people of other religious and political persuasions might become more than an unrealized fancy.

Let us then move on to an overview of Freire's life

and works. The final part of this book will present an analysis and interpretation of Freire's educational philosophy.

II

It is fortunate that Paulo Freire and others have told us about his early life.[2] He was born on September 19, 1921 in Recife, a port city of northeastern Brazil. He speaks gently and lovingly of his father, Joaquim Themistocles Freire, and of his mother, Edeltrus Neves Freire. It was they, he says, who by example and love taught him to prize dialogue and to respect the choices of others. His parents were of the middle class but suffered financial reverses so severe during the Great Depression that Freire learned what it is for a grade school child to go hungry. The family had to move in 1931 to Jabatao where his father later died. Professor Richard Shaull recounts that at this stage Freire resolved to dedicate his life "to the struggle against hunger, so that other children would not have to know the agony he was then experiencing."[3] His performance in school at the age of fifteen (two years behind his age group in the classroom) was just barely adequate to qualify him for secondary school, but after his family situation improved a bit he was able to complete school, and he entered the University of Recife where he enrolled in the Faculty of Law and also studied philosophy and the psychology of language while working part-time as an instructor of Portuguese in a secondary school. Like most adolescents he questioned the discrepancy between what he heard preached in church and what life was really like on weekdays. For about a

year's time he withdrew from the practice of Catholicism but returned to it because of the lectures of Tris-
tâo de Atayde. During this period he was reading the
works of Maritain, Bernanos, and Mounier, the Christian personalist who strongly influenced his educational
philosophy.[4]

In 1944 Freire married Elza Maia Costa Oliveira
of Recife, a grade school teacher (later a principal). She
was to bear him three daughters and two sons. Freire
says that at that time of his life his interest in theories
of education began to grow and that he was doing more
reading in education, philosophy, and the sociology of
education than in law, a discipline in which he claims
he was only an average student.[5] In fact it later turned
out that after passing the bar he quickly abandoned law
as a means of earning a living in order to go to work as
a welfare official and later as director of the Depart-
ment of Education and Culture of the Social Service in
the State of Pernambuco. His experiences during those
years of public service brought him into direct contact
with the urban poor. The educational and organiza-
tional assignments he undertook there led him to begin
to formulate the means of communicating with the dis-
possessed that would later develop into his dialogical
methodology. Involvement in adult education also included directing seminars and teaching courses in the
history and philosophy of education at the University
of Recife, where he was awarded a doctoral degree in
1959.

In the early 1960's Brazil was a restless nation.
Numerous reform movements flourished simultaneously as socialists, communists, students, labor leaders, populists, and Christian militants all sought their
own socio-political goals. At that time Brazil had a

population of some 34.5 million people of whom only 15.5 million could vote. Widespread illiteracy among the rural poor (especially in the northeast where Freire worked) served the interests of the dominant minority because eligibility for the franchise was dependent upon the ability to read and write. It is not surprising that, after the populist leader João Goulart replaced Janio Quadros as Brazil's president in 1961, peasant leagues and other popular cultural movements aimed at consciousness-raising and nation-wide literacy campaigns, such as the Basic Education Movement (MEB) sponsored by the Brazilian bishops, intensified. Through the federal government's Superintendency for the Development of the Northeast (SUDENE) under the direction of Celso Furtado, programs to assist economic development in nine states included courses and scholarships for the training of scientists and specialists. Educational aid was later planned to extend to primary and adult literacy programs in light of the special educational implications of the radical restructuring that SUDENE envisioned.[6]

It was in the midst of this ferment and heightened expectations that Paulo Freire became the first director of the University of Recife's Cultural Extension Service which brought the literacy programs now famous as the *Método Paulo Freire* to thousands of peasants in the northeast. Later, from June 1963 up to March 1964, Freire's teams worked throughout the entire nation. They claimed success in interesting adult illiterates in learning how to read and write in as short a time as forty-five days.

Why did Freire's methods enjoy rapid success? What made it appealing for *campesinos* who worked from dawn to dusk in the fields to attend sessions every

night for six to eight weeks? The answer lies in understanding the process of *conscientização* ("conscientization"), the word Freire uses to describe authentic education. In the pages to come we will have a great deal to
say about conscientization; for the time being let it be
enough to say that Freire and his co-workers were not
content simply to try to teach people to read and write.
By presenting participation in the political process
through knowledge of reading and writing as a desirable
and attainable goal for all Brazilians, Freire won the
interest of the poor and gave them the hope that they
could start to have a say in the larger issues of Brazilian
life. Peasant passivity and fatalism waned as literacy became attainable and valued. Freire's methods were in-
contestably politicizing and, in the eyes of the Brazilian
military and land-owners anxious to stave off societal
change, outrageously radical.

Fear of literacy, especially the kind of literacy
sought by Freire, is nothing new in the Americas. In the
not too distant past history of the United States of
America, the introductory paragraph to an 1831 statute
in North Carolina was worded as follows:

> Whereas the teaching of slaves to read and write
> has a tendency to excite dissatisfaction in their
> minds, and to produce insurrection and rebellion,
> to the manifest injury of this State: Therefore, be it
> enacted . . .[7]

One need quote no more to let the reader guess what
severe punishments of fines, imprisonment, and whip-
pings (the latter only for freed blacks or slaves) were
prescribed for transgressors. A similar logic reigned in
the minds of the military who overthrew the Goulart

regime in Brazil in April 1964. All populist movements were suppressed and Freire was thrown into jail for his "subversive" activities. He spent a total of seventy days there where he was repeatedly questioned and accused. In prison he began his first major educational work, *Educação como Practica da Liberdade* (*Education as the Practice of Freedom*). The book, an analysis of his failure to effect change in Brazil, had to be completed in Chile, because Freire was sent into exile.

Here I would like to pause in my account of the events of Freire's life to begin speaking about his writings and especially about his first work, *Education as the Practice of Freedom*. Up until 1973 the principal difficulty for North Americans who wished to study Freire was the relative inaccessibility of his written works. *Cultural Action for Freedom* (1970) and *Pedagogy of the Oppressed* (1970) were published here in the United States, but, with the exception of Freire's Harvard seminars attended by a privileged few in 1968-1969, those books were the only introduction to Freire's thought that the majority of American scholars had at their disposal. Not until 1973 was *Education as the Practice of Freedom* translated into English, along with another essay of his, *¿Extensión o Communicación?*[8] It is unfortunate that Freire's first American critics did not have access to his first work, because his narrative of the Brazilians' struggle for liberation and his exposition of his pedagogical methods are much richer there than in the English works mentioned above. Apart from objections to his espousals of socialism and his apparent justification of revolutionary violence in *Pedagogy of the Oppressed*, nearly all who commented about Freire took him to task for vagueness, redundancy, incredibly complex sentence structures, and

parenthetical explanations that range from a paragraph
to two or three pages in length. It was extremely difficult for them to appreciate the interplay between his
theory and methodology. *Education as the Practice of
Freedom* does a much better job of that, and I recommend it as the best introduction to his thought.

Why is Freire repetitive? More than anything else,
I believe it is due to emphasis upon dialectical thinking
which he insists must begin in the total experience of
human beings. Freire maintains that philosophical reflection cannot be divorced from time, space, or the
consciousness of human subjects who act upon reality.
When trying to expose his ideas or to discuss the dis-
tinction of mankind from the world of things and animals, Freire constantly draws attention to the dialectical interplay of reality and human consciousness
along with the infinite number of influences acting simultaneously and successively to determine history and
consciousness. This focus, along with cautious, Hus-
serlian explanations of the multifaceted phenomenon of
human consciousness, inevitably invites repetition.

Education as the Practice of Freedom presents a
philosophical view of what men and women are capable
of becoming when enabled to transform history and
become subjects through a process of critical reflection.
Freire contrasts the "ontological possibility" of every
person's becoming a subject with the people of Brazil
who began as a colonized, closed society in which
power was first exercised by those who exploited Brazil
only to return to Portugal, then by estate-lords who
ruled enormous plantations which offered protection
and subsistence-level support to the serfs and slaves
who worked there. The two early Brazilian societies
were characterized by paternalism: on the part of the

slaves and serfs a "culture of silence" emerged in which they had no dialogue with their masters; on the part of the elites, power oscillated in struggles between estate-lords and the governors. The rise of cities occasioned by the life of the royal family in Rio in the early nineteenth century saw a "Europeanization" of Brazilian culture with power no longer the exclusive possession of rural oligarchs. There was, however, still no participation of the masses in the legislature. Only land owners and the wealthy urban elites had political rights; the rest of Brazilian society, by far the majority, remained marginalized.

During the past two centuries Brazil tried to import the structure of a national democratic state. In Freire's judgment this was an uncritical solution, typical of an alienated culture, naive and "messianic" because Brazilian society was without the conditions necessary for the critical construction of a democracy. The people of Brazil witnessed establishment of a republic, the abolition of slavery, the growth of industry in the last part of the nineteenth century, and the rapid expansion of industrial society during the 1920's and 1930's (which continued at an even faster pace after World War II) as a culture of silence. These alterations in the national life brought Brazil in the twentieth century into a state of transition that Freire calls a "crash" between centuries-old inexperience with democracy and new problems of growth, development, and planning that do not lend themselves to humane solutions without participation of the masses they affect.

For such a society in transition, a mode of education providing profound political reforms, not just new techniques and economic structures, was necessary to assure the basis and establishment of democracy. An essential note of democracy is change mandated by decisions of the people. Freire therefore asserted that education must be social and political, a constant attempt to change one's attitudes and create democratic dispositions. As an adult educator in Brazil, Freire saw that his work was not confined to overcoming illiteracy; it resolved itself into the task of also overcoming Brazilian inexperience in democracy. The methodology he chose in literacy programs attempted to perform both tasks simultaneously. Freire was severely critical of tradidtional Brazilian education for its fondness for memorization and rhetorical skill, and for its failure to teach people to be critical. He also criticized Brazilian intellectuals and accused them of thinking and writing from European or North American viewpoints and of failing to criticize society and to educate from a Brazilian point of view.

The last chapter of *Education as the Practice of Freedom*, entitled "Education and Conscientization," describes the various phases of the problem-posing methodology that Freire and his teams utilized in Brazil. An appendix also provides sketches of illustrations used by Freire's teams who "codified" man's relationships with the world and then presented them to the peasants for discussion.[9] The discussions provided "generative words" (e.g., *shanty, well, work, plow, slum, school*) for the people to study as they began to read and write. Generative words were always selected as a result of investigation and discussion of life in each locale. They were termed *generative* for two reasons: (1) because they could prompt discussion of familiar matters of daily importance to the illiterates, and (2) because in Romance languages polysyllabic words can easily be broken down into their syllabic components and used to form new words. By means of highly charged generative words, peasants quickly learned to read and to spell. But Freire did not confine his method to a mere transfer of skills. The generative words indicated real-life situations of man in relation to the world around him, and thus a word like *favela* (slum) was not utilized to teach people just to read the syllables *fa-fe-fi-fo-fu, va-ve-vi-vo-vu, la-le-li-lo-lu* and to see the possibility of combining these little word blocks to form new words. The picture of a slum, along with discussion of slum life, introduced new "generative themes" and new words to read and write which directed peasant attention to problems of housing, diet, clothing, health, education, and so forth. In turn, the themes illustrated human life and culture as problems to be solved by the people: hunger, dependence, unemployment, and so forth. Descriptions of Freire's methodology abound in many languages, put together by many authors. I am still convinced that his own work in "Education and Conscientization" is the best material capable of enlightening the inquirer about the origins of his method.

After his expulsion from Brazil, Freire worked in Chile for five years with the adult education programs of the Eduardo Frei government headed by Waldemar Cortes who attracted international attention and UNESCO acknowledgement that Chile was one of the five nations of the world which had best succeeded in overcoming illiteracy. His work there was not confined to literacy campaigns. Frei's Christian Democratic government was also interested in agrarian reform. Freire was able to continue to promote his educational ideas, addressing the problems of Chilean adult education in two works, *Sobre la Acción Cultural* and the essay *¿Extensión o Communicación?*

One notes in Freire's Chilean experiences a special

importance regarding the first phase of the "Paulo Freire Method," the thorough investigation of the culture and customs that shape the lives of illiterates. He had to work not only with a different language in Chile, but with completely different kinds of urban and rural illiterates. Thomas Sanders has well described the deeply contextual orientation of Freire's method as well as some of the more significant adaptations he had to make after his move to Chile.[10] Freire learned that in contrast to Brazil where illiterates had been readily interested in discussions about their lives, about human nature and the nature of knowing, the Chilean peasant tended to lose interest if he did not begin to learn immediately. Freire had to start all over again in studying the first steps and devising generative words. The pictures and slides he used in Chile also had generative words superimposed upon the codification of rural culture. This had not been done in Brazil.

With regard to the problems of illiteracy and agrarian reform, something ought to be said here about the books he produced in Chile. In the case of literacy training, Freire had no use for traditional primers whose simple sentences were irrelevant to the illiterates because of their triviality. More importantly, he rejected Brazilian and Chilean primers because they imposed cultural values of the middle and wealthy classes upon the peasants. (The title of the primer his teams used in Brazil, *Viver é Lutar [To Live Is To Struggle]* suggests a provocative generative theme all by itself. Freire used a similar primer entitled *Communidad [Community]* in the Chilean programs.) In Chile, Freire became a critic of traditional extension education because he found it guilty of modernizing without developing. One of the generative themes running throughout his writings is that "all development is modernization, but not all modernization is equal to development."[11]

Sobre la Acción Cultural discusses the problems of cultural change which go hand in hand with teaching and learning new skills. The essays in the book were intended as pedagogical aids to facilitate cultural change by humanizing the agrarian reform. To my knowledge *Sobre la Acción Cultural* is the first written work in which Freire identifies traditional education as "banking" education. The latter is a deliberately chosen metaphor by which he accuses all who disagree with his concept of humanistic education of being paternalistic exploiters, willing to teach skills or to change social patterns only insofar as they will receive a return on their investment. In the first hundred pages of the book Freire gives the outline of what a liberating humanistic education is. The same themes are elaborated in all his subsequent works. *Sobre la Acción Cultural* is the first book in which he names his pedagogy "cultural action for freedom"—a phrase used later as the title of one of the books he wrote in the United States.

Freire demands that learning be a dialogical process of the investigation of reality. Literacy programs might be very dramatic instances of liberating education, but cultural action for freedom is not confined to the first stage of providing people with their rights. Traditional banking education contrasts sharply with dialogue, which never dichotomizes man from the world, subject from object, or teacher from student. Humanizing education is preeminently dialogical, a constant co-investigation carried out by students who recognize that knowing is a process of never-ending perception, and by educators who recognize that they are themselves students.

He argues that dialogical cultural action can create the possibility of real cultural change because investigation of cultural reality discovers antagonistic contradictions inherent in any social system. (A Marxist premise is evident in his assertion that the key to humanizing agrarian reforms is education that recognizes the dialectical nature of reality.) Conditioned as it is by social contradictions, education should be a process involving three dialectical moments: investigation of thinking, thematization (by means of generative words and other codifications), and problematization of social reality.

Problematization provokes new moments in the dialectical process. Freire terms these "limit situations" (new comprehensions of reality demanding protest, situations which must be transcended and transformed to accomplish liberation) and "generative themes"—so termed because from investigation and discovery of the people's thematic universe new themes are constantly evoked which again present themselves as historical reality and tasks to be accomplished in the process of liberation. The process of liberation is never complete; it always demands new investigation, thematization, and problematization.

Other essays in *Sobre la Acción Cultural* speak more directly to agrarian reform. Employment of methods of banking education by simply filling *campesinos* with technical knowledge while ignoring the determinants and conditioning of culture defeats the intention of land reform. Similarly, attempts to reduce men to mere producers in order to increase their productivity is dehumanizing education, because increase in production is not the purpose of man's existence. It is only a limited end of the agrarian reforms. Social workers should be agents of change whose principal task is demythologizing reality with the goal of setting it as a problem for the peasants. Professionals, men who possess expert knowledge, must realize the non-neutrality of technology and commit themselves to humanization of land reforms by commitment to the goals of cultural change.

¿Extensión o Communicación? proceeds as a semantic inquiry into implications of the two words provided as educational alternatives in the book's title. Extension programs err when they disseminate information if they only show people objectified, "extended" knowledge without revealing or unveiling the reality of man-world relationships. Ignoring or minimizing the philosophical problem of man's nature and how he learns is, in Freire's view, suicidal to the intent of land reform. Peasants, conditioned by history and society to think of themselves as things (objects), not as men (subjects), as parts of nature like plants and animals (objects), may learn bits of information (also objects) in the sense that animals can be trained, but they do not possess real knowledge. Only subjects (men and women) can know in the true sense because only subjects can be aware of their perceptions and of their knowledge as problematic. Extension programs that continue to treat people as objects are doomed to failure unless they make their primary objective the establishment of permanent relationships with the *campesinos* a relationship between subjects.

The real task of the agronomist educator is to approach campesinos in a loving, humble manner that will assist them to liberate themselves from "magical" thinking and dependence upon priests and rituals, or from "naive" consciousness about political reforms. The work will be accomplished to the extent that educators stress the role of *campesinos* as that of men and women who are co-responsible for the creation and implementation of political decisions. Conscientization cannot be anti-dialogical; it does not manipulate or reify the peasants. Successful "extension" has to be "communication." The serious problems of planting, soil care, reforestation, and so forth are in many parts of Latin America governed by patterns of belief. So too is peasant behavior. Experts who overlook the cultural attitudes of peasants by transplanting knowledge overlook the fact that their own skills are also products of culture. One culture cannot be extended on top of another culture without domestication by means of "cultural invasion." Freire called intersubjectivity the key to unlocking the world of culture and history for the agronomists and *campesinos* alike. Once people search together as knowing subjects, they should come to realize that education cannot be anti-dialogical without being anti-scientific and oppressing.

Toward the end of the 1960's, Freire's work brought him into contact with a new culture that changed his thought significantly. At the invitation of Harvard University he left Latin America to come to the United States where he taught as Visiting Professor at Harvard's Center for Studies in Education and Development and was also Fellow at the Center for the Study of Development and Social Change. Those years were, of course, a period of violent unrest in the United States when opposition to the country's involvement in Southeast Asia brought police and militias onto university campuses. Racial unrest had since 1965 flared into violence on the streets of American cities. Minority spokesmen and war protesters were publishing and teaching, and they influenced Freire profoundly. His reading of the American scene was an awakening to him because he found that repression and exclusion of the powerless from economic and political life was not limited to third world countries and cultures of dependence. He extended his definition of the third world from a geographical concern to a political concept,[12] and the theme of violence became a greater preoccupation in his writings from that time on.

In 1969-1970 he published two articles for the *Harvard Educational Review* entitled "Adult Literacy Process as Cultural Action for Freedom" and "Cultural Action and Conscientization." The two papers summarized for the first time in English most of his educational theories previously elaborated in Portuguese and Spanish works. The same articles were also released in a joint publication of the *Harvard Educational Review* and the Center for the Study of Development and Social Change in a booklet entitled *Cultural Action for Freedom*. The booklet contains an introduction written by Freire reflecting his view that themes of alienation, domination, and oppression typifying the world of illiterates and the landless are found within cultures of total silence and also within sub-cultures of the first world. The work restates his thesis that no education can be neutral and that education ought to be cultural action for freedom. In a brief appendix he provided English readers a few examples taken from literacy education programs to clarify use of terms such as "generative words," "codifications" and "de-codifications" that had previously baffled readers who were unaware of the origins of Freire's pedagogy in a matrix of literacy schooling for adults.

Cultural Action for Freedom was followed shortly by the English translation of his most famous book,

Pedagogy of the Oppressed. I have already mentioned some difficulties that Americans who were unfamiliar with Freire's Brazilian experience found in the book. Critics like Edgar Friedenburg who called it a "wooden translation" and a "truly bad book" were harsh.[13] Unfavorable reviewers tended to agree that Freire had painted an oversimplified, excessively black and white picture of socio-political reality. His critique of the oppressive tendencies and failures of traditional education was generally accepted, but he was faulted by many readers for a too ready approval of revolutionary violence as the only solution to oppressive education. He was accused of being ambiguous, a mythmaker, and impractical, and of being an oppressor himself. In addition he was severely criticized for his lack of originality. David Harmon's observation that Freire's justification of violence in the name of liberation was so considerable that it obscured his other contributions to education does seem to hit the mark.[14]

Nevertheless the work is a development of his earlier writings, and one finds in it an excellent exposition of the tactics of manipulative educators. The book elaborates Freire's basic theme: men and women, to be fully human, must become subjects. Education that fails to enhance the "ontological vocation" of mankind is not only non-neutral, it is suffocating. From the very beginning it is clear that Freire wants to talk about education and the poor of this world who are victims of oppression. If education is to succeed it will be a process of humanization carried out *by* and *with*, not *for* the larger part of mankind. The existence of dependent cultures is necessary (but dialectically opposed) to the existence of dominant elites who possess political and economic power. Dominated peoples are the oppressed, and while it may be true that they happen to be poor, they are not specifically differentiated by poverty but by their deprivation of the right to determine their own history.

Freire introduces the need for a pedagogy of the oppressed. Education is to be the path to permanent liberation and admits of two stages. The first stage is that by which men become aware (conscientized) of their oppression and through praxis transform that state. The second stage builds upon the first and is a permanent process of liberating cultural action.

Freire defines violence as any action (whether it involves physical brutality or not) that denies men their humanity and self-determination. The situation defining a class of mankind as oppressed is the one in which violence is initiated by the oppressor class. With responsibility for violence laid solely at the door of oppressors, libertarian action (education, rebellion, revolution) is not an outbreak of violence begun by the oppressed but a legitimate response to the oppressors' violence. In the most objectionable section of the book he leaves himself wide open for attack by claiming that this "liberating action" may be paradoxically termed a "gesture of love."[15]

The bulk of the work addresses educational themes treated in *Sobre la Acción Cultural:* banking education, problem-posing, the nature of men, the teacher-student contradiction, dialogical education, and investigation of generative themes. Freire added a final chapter which is the most practical section of the book. He contrasts cultural action for freedom and cultural action for domestication to provide understanding of the tactics of oppressors and examples of the pedagogy he recommends to revolutionary leadership. Anti-dialogical education is characterized by conquest, division and rule of the people, manipulation by elites, and cultural invasion which educates people to be objects. On the other hand dialogical revolutionary pedagogy seeks the polar opposites of each of the oppressor tactics mentioned in the last sentence: cooperation with the people, unity, organization of the people to attain freely chosen goals, and finally cultural synthesis.

Another article that Freire produced in 1970 ought to be mentioned in connection with *Pedagogy of the Oppressed*. If critics justly took him to task elsewhere for ambiguity and style, "The Political Literacy Process—An Introduction" should make amends.[16] In a very few pages he was able to summarize his theories, developing the implications of the power to read and write. He utilized the metaphor of "political literacy" to describe all education as a process whereby men and women become liberated. Even though an individual may have spent years in schools and universities, if he has only received "deposits" of education to domesticate him he is still politically "illiterate," incapable of "reading" human existence in a manner that allows him to transcend the limit situation that maintains oppression. A few succinct paragraphs review and illustrate Freire's notions of what a human being is, human consciousness, critical reflection, and cultural action for freedom. If earlier works left readers unprepared to state precisely what Freire enunciates as the goal of education, this little monograph is unequivocal: men and women ought to learn to read and write by becoming politicized and then radicalized in a permanent process of liberation.

For the past five years Freire has remained in exile from Brazil, making his home with his wife in Geneva.

Most if not all of his children are now married. He serves as Special Educational Consultant to the World Council of Churches and has spent the first half of the 1970's traveling all over the world lecturing and devoting his efforts to assisting educational programs of newly independent countries in Asia and Africa, such as Tanzania. He also serves as chairman of the executive committee of the *Institut d'Action Culturelle* (IDAC) which is headquartered in Geneva. IDAC is a nonprofit organization formed by people who wish to pursue through study and experimentation the possibility of education through conscientization. In addition to undertaking research and sponsoring workshops and other programs involving conscientization, IDAC has continued since 1973 to publish a series of documents promoting Freire's ideas and applying them to liberation issues around the globe.

For a number of reasons Paulo Freire continues to be the center of controversy. We shall see that his philosophical eclecticism is unsatisfying to many. Others complain that, in spite of the success of his literacy methods, he has failed to offer any clear practical program for liberation capable of transfer to other environments.

Radicals have criticized Freire too. His insistence on dialogue, they say, might paralyze a revolution. (Stalin learned a long time ago that bullets were far more persuasive than dialogue when he wanted to industrialize the Soviet Union.) People have invited him to assist with educational planning and then have become frustrated when he has refused to offer prefabricated solutions (he would call them "prescriptions") for their difficulties. In fairness, the reader should understand that Freire has never pretended to possess "the answer," and I am certain, from his previous experiences with people who impose plans or decisions, that he would fear any single person claiming a role of pedagogical messiahship. Unlike doctrinaire Marxists, Freire genuinely believes that respect for people and open dialogue can lead to a more humane, a more just world. Faced with the diversity and complexities of the myriad liberation movements in many lands, one simply cannot expect to find final solutions from Freire or anyone else. That expectation is what he would call an example of "naive consciousness" in the extreme.

What of educators in "developed" nations? Can Freire be dismissed by them as irrelevant? Hardly. Even if one grants that his written works are confusing, and that he is at times oversimplified and incomplete, his devastating criticisms of traditional education and oppression by political brawn or mere bureaucratic intrasigence cannot be neglected. He is a gadfly in the best Socratic tradition and speaks to every educator. Those who teach or work in Christian schools should have special difficulty in turning a deaf ear to Freire, unless they prefer an educational praxis other than what their churches preach.

III

Up to this point we have presented the barest outline of the main events of Freire's life and situated his writings in the context of his career and the tasks which faced him in Brazil and Chile and the United States. At first, his life story might be all that appears necessary to understand why his pedagogy is called a "pedagogy of liberation." Christians familiar with the writings of

Dietrich Bonhoeffer, Karl Rahner, the history and subsequent developments of the Second Vatican Council and liberation theologies are not surprised to find a Catholic like Freire calling into question in a very fundamental way the failure of traditional education to produce Christian citizens who can function as effective critics and change agents in contemporary society. The various theologies of liberation emanating for the most part from Latin American thinkers like Juan Luis Segundo, Gustavo Gutierrez, Rubem Alves and others are all in agreement that the churches must address themselves to problems of the here and now. Moreover the popularity of a Marxist critique of society with the Catholic Left in Latin America is surprising only to those who know nothing of the starvation, unemployment, and oppression of the peoples who constitute the third world. Assuredly, there are excesses evident in the thought of some, but the compassion and eagerness of liberation theologians to fulfill a Christian prophetic role lead one to agree with Bonaventure Kloppenburg that the "central concerns [of theologies of liberation] are completely legitimate and fully Christian."[17]

To read Freire and come away with the notion that he is "merely another neo-Marxist" is to sell him short. While it is true that his analysis of history and culture leans heavily on the thought of Marx and Mao, of Fanon, Lukacs, Althusser, and Marcuse, his educational philosophy does not lend itself to quick analysis or identification with any specific school. His thinking flows from his life experiences and is eclectic, a synthesis of many strains of thought which do indeed lead him to the conclusion that education must lead to political liberation. Because of his syncretism he has been called an idealist, a communist, a "theologian in disguise," a phenomenologist, and an existentialist. Freire's ability to draw upon so many varied and rich developments probably accounts for his widespread popularity and the fascination he arouses among people of curiously different, if not antagonistic, viewpoints. His colleagues at the *Institut d'Action Culturelle* have drawn attention to Freire's particolored philosophy and the effect it has on his readership:

Freire has a very large reader public. But the thought which one meets in his writings demands a great deal of awareness so as to be assimilated. It constitutes a synthesis which is difficult to grasp in its totality. Therefore, every reader runs the risk of retaining only those points which directly concern him or her or those issues which are understandable because of his or her points of reference. The Latin American reader understands Freire because of an experience of political struggle or an involvement in a social movement which has a socio-economic framework. The Catholic reader identifies with Freire's humanist orientation and feels on familiar ground with Freire and the philosophers who have influenced him. The Marxist reader recognizes in Freire's writings a number of contemporary currents which Marxist thinkers (Gramsci, Lukacs, Marcuse) are used to dealing with. The reader who happens to be an educator finds accents of liberation which characterize progressive tendencies in the contemporary pedagogical debate. Only those who are, in part, all of these people at once or who have, in their own history, passed by way of these different "stages" and been submitted to these different "influences" can grasp the totality of Freire's intellectual development.[18]

I surely make no claim to have passed through all the different stages of Freire's life, and it would be more than arrogance to pretend to have grasped the totality of his intellectual development. His work and study on many continents enable him to quote at will from scores of philosophers, psychologists, sociologists, political scientists, educators, revolutionaries, and theologians. It is possible, however, to identify some of the major accents in his writings and the personalities whose thought to a greater or less degree contributed to his philosophy.

Let me begin by again drawing attention to Latin America as the geographical font of Freire's thought. The history of Brazil and its evolution from colonialism, the struggle of the masses against government by a powerful few, and finally dependence upon foreign capital and foreign economies in the twentieth century is not much different from the histories of other countries in Latin America. In both Brazil and the Spanish-speaking nations, European culture, values, and religion have been assimilated and fused with indigenous Indian cultures. Today European hegemony has been replaced by North American influences, but the situation of dependence of Latin America upon foreign cultures has not changed. Paulo Freire was born into a culture of dependence that is much more than an economic and political reality. The literature, art, religion, and family customs of Latin America are a blend of European and native American patterns of living that color Freire's understanding of *conscientização*.

European philosophy, beginning with the Greek tradition of love for human freedom and the Christian humanism of the Middle Ages, would be a natural starting point for the Brazilian student of philosophy. And it seems that in spite of evolution of his thought

amid the harshness of oppressed Latin American societies, Freire never has divorced himself from concepts of
human nature found early in Western philosophy. John
Donohue drew attention to some fundamental notions
in Freire's thought:

> To begin with, Freire fully accepts the Greek (and
> Christian) concept of man as a being essentially
> defined by the powers of reflective thought and
> free choice. For him, as for Aristotle, knowledge
> and liberty are the true goods of the soul. We are
> most human when we are free and most free when
> we can choose. Freire, as his work and writings
> show, is dominated by the desire to make these
> humanistic values fully available to everyone. He
> is consequently critical of both capitalist and Com-
> munist societies because he believes that neither
> allows for the maximum self-development and
> growth in freedom of all men and women.[19]

Of course these ideas are not restricted to "classical"
humanism; one finds them exalted in existentialist
thought and recurrent in other philosophies. With re-
strictions on thought and freedom of choice and expression a daily reality in Latin America, one is not surprised to discover an eagerness in Freire to turn
classical ideals into practically applicable pedagogy. He
was able to do this by uniting the observations and
reflections of a number of modern and contemporary
thinkers into his own philosophy of education. It is impossible here to account for every single person who
shaped his ideas, but I believe it useful to single out five
philosophical strains which combine with Freire's classical humanism to shape his thought. They are (1) per-

sonalism, especially as evidenced in the writings of Emmanuel Mounier; (2) existentialism; (3) phenomenology; (4) Marxism; (5) Christianity. Spokesmen from each of these quarters convinced Freire that the world is not an eternal *given* and that there is a possibility of men acting to eliminate alienation from one another and from their Creator. I will say a few words about each of these influences with the hope that discussion in the paragraphs to follow will make the analysis of Freire's thought in the final section of this book more readily intelligible.

Personalism. We mentioned above that early in his intellectual development Freire was reading the works of Emmanuel Mounier. Mounier, a French intellectual prominent in the Resistance against Hitler, was until the time of his death in 1950 editor of the journal *L'Espirit.* He was a Catholic critic both of traditional Christianity and of European rationalism. Like Freire after him, he was a controversial figure. When Mounier advocated practical policies he came close to alliance with the French Communists in the post-war period.[20] He viewed with dismay the reaction of those who blamed the shattering of European society upon the machine age and scolded those Christians who fled from the challenge of remaking the world. In the introduction to the English translation of Mounier's *Be Not Afraid* Leslie Paul tells us that Mounier sought "to prove that the impulse to remake the world, which receives so much Christian disapproval, has a Christian origin."[21] Many of the themes found in Mounier's philosophy of history are to be found later in Freire: that history has a meaning, that in spite of wars and other disasters history drives toward the betterment and liberation of mankind, that science and technology are welcome developments in this drive of history toward amelioration, that man has a "glorious mission of being the agent of his own liberation."[22] Mounier stressed the theme and the tasks of re-creation remaining for Christians to make visible the spiritual activity of their Creator. He also wrote of the dangers of a technology left unhumanized. Mounier's personalism was friendly to Marx, ambiguous in its effort to foster Christian collectivism, and thoroughly opposed to the restoration of nineteenth-century individualism or totalitarian states. Personalism was not a political system or even a complete philosophy. It was a perspective, an optimistic way of looking at the world and a summons to action that indelibly stamped the chracter of Freire's thought.

Existentialism. Throughout his writings Freire quotes from Sartre, Jaspers, Marcel, Heidegger, Camus, Buber, and many others who come under the general classification of existentialist thinkers. The specific influence of each philosopher upon Freire is well nigh impossible to trace, but one may still identify concerns and values in Freire which derive from existentialist philosophy. His passion for "true acts of knowing," for authenticity in education, for "authentic" and "inauthentic" states of existence, and for freedom for men and women to become subjects—such are existentialist preoccupations. Above all, the emphasis that Freire places upon dialogue as an essential tool in his methodology and as a criterion for judgment of the degree to which oppression or openness typifies a given political structure evidences the extent to which Freire esteems intersubjectivity.

Existentialist emphasis upon man's freedom to choose and to act takes the form in many authors of demythologizing the reasons why a person or a society chooses specific goals, values, economic structures, or forms of government. Freire's methodology proceeds by discussion of the reasons why people feel constrained in their choices or think of themselves as beings-for-others rather than as free beings-for-themselves. Among modern educators or psychological theoreticians like Carl Rogers, one also discerns a hunger for personal assimilation of knowledge and values rather than mastery of bare facts. Existentialist educators want knowing to become important not of itself or on the say-so of others, but by one's deliberate decision to know and become skilled. Freire's contrast of "banking education" with "true acts of knowing" certainly matches the existentialist assault on traditional schools in the name of personal freedom.

Phenomenology. The very term *conscientization* and the attention Freire pays to human states of consciousness have often exposed him to the charge that he is an idealist, a dreamer who seeks to change social reality by a simple change of human consciousness. Others like Peter Berger have interpreted conscientization as a mere consciousness-raising technique.[23] It is fair to say that the necessity for reflection upon one's consciousness and group consciousness is an essential feature in Freire's thought and methodology. But his concern with consciousness is more basic than a desire to change other people's consciousness. From Husserl's phenomenological method he adopts the principle that exploration of consciousness is a prerequisite to knowledge of reality, and it enables the knower to study reality when fully intent upon what appears to the perceiving subject. Husserl also held that consciousness is able to reflect upon itself so as to know its own structure, consciousness of self. Freire uses a phenomenological investigation of reality and consciousness itself in order to unveil the mode of human knowing. This is done so that he and his students can come to discover themselves as a part of reality, distinct from the reality which is not that of a knowing subject, and capable of examining it. Although his penchant for philosophizing about consciousness in his written works irritates many critics, in practice his probing of human consciousness and appearances leads to discovery of (1) the social conditioning of consciousness and (2) the power of thinking subjects to act on their own behalf.

Marxism. The story of Freire's life makes intelligible his attraction to a Marxist interpretation of history and culture. DeWitt[24] and others have pointed out that Freire may be guilty of contradiction in his classical notion of man as a radically free being and his acceptance of a dialectical or Hegelian view of man espoused by Marx. Freire is more roundly condemned, as we have seen, for his too ready approval of revolutionary violence in *Pedagogy of the Oppressed.* But Freire is a Latin American, and the contrasts which exist there between the rich and the destitute, the powerful and the powerless, make it difficult to see life as much else than a struggle for the larger part of humanity.[25] Whatever the weaknesses by oversimplification of history, economics, and sociology in Marx and the socialist thinkers after him quoted so often by Freire, dialectical thinking is prompted and stimulated in an environment where contrasts are so painfully evident. It is easy for educators to discuss the liberal arts in the comfort of a university; it is far more practical to talk about liberating arts in a village with muddy streets populated by hungry people without shoes.

For all his revolutionary rhetoric, Freire's radicalism remains divorced from any specific political system. That is no doubt why his appeal remains popular. Freire admits that he does not have all the answers but believes that if people are once allowed freedom, they can work out political systems responsive to their needs. Education must be directed toward political action, but Freire is loath to say what form that action must take beyond a vague socialism.

Christianity. Born into Catholicism, Freire decided as an adult to practice his faith, but in far from a traditional manner (insofar as the "tradition" in Latin American societies has aligned a majority of churchmen with reactionary forces). The tradition of Freire is the tradition of the Old Testament prophets and of Christ who presented thorny questions such as the hunger, thirst, and nakedness of one's neighbors in terms that rule out indifference on the part of disciples. Freire has patience with neither traditionalist nor modernizing churches; he is fascinated with the prospect of a Church that practices what it preaches and believes that the new theologies may restore a fundamental Christian urgency to social reform in Latin America and elsewhere.[26]

Freire says that notions of God can paralyze human activity by depicting the world and social contradictions as situations which are decreed from eternity. The person who tries to explain social injustice to himself or to others as the will of God flounders in a false Christianity:

Normally, he [the individual trying to understand his oppression] will try to size up his situation. He will look for the causes, the reasons for his condition, in things higher and more powerful than man. One such thing is God, whom he sees as the

maker, the cause of his condition. Ah, but if God
is responsible, man can do nothing. Many Christians today, thanks be to God, are vigorously
reacting against that attitude, especially in Brazil.
But as a child, I knew many priests who went out
to the peasants saying: "Be patient. This is God's
will. And anyway, it will earn heaven for you."
Yet the truth of the matter is that we have to earn
our heaven here and now, we ourselves. We have
to build our heaven, to fashion it during our lifetime, right now. This latter sort of theology is a
very passive one that I cannot stomach.

How could we make God responsible for the ca-
lamity? As if Absolute Love could abandon man to
constant victimization and total destitution. That
would be a God such as Marx described.[27]

At first reading the above quotation might cause a person to ask "Is Freire a Pelagian? Does he say man can
save himself?" The answer to the first question is *no*.
Recall that Mounier, Freire, Teilhard de Chardin and
others view Christianity as a call to cooperate in the
task of redemption. The Christian who confines his
practice of faith to church attendance or complete passivity (in the sense that it becomes fatalism) fails to be
fully Christian. Freire wants Christians to enter into active relationships with the world in the name of the liberation preached by Christ. With regard to the second
question, man can never be entirely responsible for his
own salvation, but the establishment of a church or the
development of the passive theologies that Freire criticizes should not chain men and women forever to a
state of inertia.

We shall see later that certain definitely Christian themes and metaphors shape the philosophy of Paulo Freire. A cynical interpretation of his use of Christian concepts and symbols in radical pedagogy no doubt says "Ah, here is Freire, another subversive wolf in sheep's clothing! He uses Christianity to trick the peasants and gain their trust." But that is just cynicism and no more. Freire operates in history, his thought has its origins in history, and Christianity is a preeminently historical development. As such it is capable of degeneration, complacency, and idle ritual. But it is also capable of *reform*. Freire is a Christian deeply committed to extrication of the oppressed from circumstances which condemn them to lives that are less than human. His repeated plea for dialogue with the oppressed has earned him criticism from revolutionaries who have no qualms about imposing solutions and plans for liberation on others without their consent. I am sure that it would be easier for him to join the ranks of atheistic revolutionaries than remain affiliated with the Catholic Church and the World Council of Churches. The fact that he remains a believer, more Christian than many of us who close our eyes to instances of social injustice, gives the lie to those who believe that his optimism is founded exclusively in politics. He is not cut off from hope, nor will he refrain from searching.

Paulo Freire is at this writing fifty-five years old. During his lifetime he has had first-hand knowledge of poverty, hunger, success, repression, and exile. Today he continues on a pilgrim's journey, lecturing, writing, and listening, prodding and encouraging people to do what they must in their own countries to bring about a more humane social order. People who listen to him and read his works more often than not find his optimism contagious: new modes of life are within our grasp to the extent we are willing to risk education as this Brazilian defines it, *cultural action for freedom.*

NOTES

1. Rosiska Darcy de Oliveira and Pierre Dominicé, *Freire/Illich—The Oppression of Pedagogy and the Pedagogy of the Oppressed* (Geneva: Institute of Cultural Action, 1975), pp. 30-33.

2. My chief sources for this section are an article written by Freire "Paulo Freire par lui-même," from *Conscientisation: Recherche de Paulo Freire* (Paris: Institut Oecumenique au Service du Developpement des Peuples, 1971), pp. 10-12, and the monograph of César Jérez and Juan Hernández Pico, "Paulo Freire y la Educación," *Estudios Centro Americanos*, XXVI, No. 274 (Aug.-Sept. 1971), pp. 498-539.

3. Richard Shaull, author of the Foreword to *Pedagogy of the Oppressed* (New York: Herder and Herder, 1972), p. 10.

4. Paulo Freire, *art. cit.*, p. 11.

5. *Ibid.*

6. John J. DeWitt, "An Exposition and Analysis of Paulo Freire's Radical Psycho-Social Andragogy of Development" (unpublished Ed.D. dissertation, School of Education, Boston University, 1971), pp. 51-53. Limitation of space does not allow me to pursue in detail all the popular attempts to bring about social reform in Brazil during this stage of Freire's career. Others have done this elsewhere and I refer the interested reader to DeWitt's excellent treatment in the first three chapters of his dissertation. Another important work for the student of this period in Brazilian history is Emmanuel DeKadt's *Catholic Radicals in Brazil* (London: Oxford University Press, 1970). DeKadt explores the origins of the Movement for Basic Education, Catholic Populism in Brazil during the years 1958-1964, and the history of the MEB since the coup of 1964.

7. *Acts Passed by the General Assembly of the State of North Carolina at the Session of 1830-1831.* (Raleigh, 1831), p. 11, quoted by Leslie H. Fishel and Benjamin Quarles, *The Negro American* (New York: Scott, Foresman and Co., 1967), p. 115.

8. These works were published in one volume: Paulo Freire, *Education for Critical Consciousness* (New York: Seabury Press, 1973).

9. These sketches, drawn by Vicente de Abreu, had to be drawn from memory of paintings originally done by Francisco Brenand. The paintings, photographed and then duplicated on slides and filmstrips, typified the everyday life and work of Brazilian peoples. Discussion of the pictures with the illiterates in "cultural circles" (Freire dislikes calling them *classes*) provoked conversations on the nature of human beings, culture, education, the nature of knowing, and the differences between rich and poor. The original paintings were confiscated by the Brazilian military who even went so far as to destroy thousands of slide projectors used by Freire and his teams! Through the kindness of Dr. Harriet Sherwin of Belvedere, California, I received copies of the slides of Brenand's paintings. On several occasions since then I have had opportunities to use the slides when discussing Freire's work with university students and am always amazed at the explosive questions and problems that students discover in these codifications.

10. Thomas G. Sanders, "The Paulo Freire Method: Literacy Training and Conscientization," *American Universities Field Staff Report*, West Coast South America Series, XV, No. 1 (Chile, 1968), pp. 1-18.

11. Freire has taken the churches in Latin America to task for too readily modernizing their procedures without making a serious attempt to work for the development of the peoples. See Paulo Freire, "The Educational Role of the Churches in Latin America," *Pasos*, No. 9 (Oct., 1972). Reprinted in edited form in Latin American Documentation Series of the U.S. Catholic Conference (LADOC), III, No. 14 (Dec. 1972), 1-14.

12. Darcy de Oliveira and Dominicé, *op. cit.*, p. 25.

13. Edgar Z. Friedenburg, "Review of *Pedagogy of the*

38 PAULO FREIRE

Oppressed," Comparative Education Review, XV, No. 3 (Oct. 1971), p. 378.

14. David Harmon, "Methodology for Revolution," *Saturday Review*, LIV, No. 25 (June 19, 1971), pp. 54-55.

15. Paulo Freire, *Pedagogy of the Oppressed* (New York: Herder and Herder, 1970), pp. 40-42.

16. Paulo Freire, "The Political Literacy Process—An Introduction" (unpublished manuscript translation of an article prepared for publication in the *Luterische Monatshefte,* Hannover, Germany, Oct. 1970).

17. Bonaventure Kloppenburg, *Temptations for the Theology of Liberation* (Chicago: Franciscan Herald Press, 1974), p. 7. Kloppenburg's thoughtful essay is a sympathetic and welcome corrective to difficulties raised by some theoreticians of the theologies of liberation. The pitfalls against which he cautions (e.g., recourse to violence, unjust prophetic denunciation, etc.) may rightly be said to be problematic in Freire's thought and pedagogy.

18. Darcy de Oliveira and Dominicé, *op. cit.*, pp. 31f. To those unfamiliar with Marx and others after him who have elaborated philosophies of praxis, Freire recommends a book by Adolfo Sanchez Vazquez, *Filosofía de la Praxis* (México, D.F.: Editorial Grijalbo, S.A., 1967).

19. John W. Donohue, "Paulo Freire—Philosopher of Adult Education," *America* CXXVII, No. 7 (Sept. 16, 1972), p. 168.

20. Donald Wolf, "Emmanuel Mounier: A Catholic of the Left," *Review of Politics*, XXII (1960), p. 333.

21. Leslie Paul, in his Foreword to Mounier's *Be Not Afraid*, translated by Cynthia Rowland (New York: Sheed & Ward, 1960), p. xv.

22. Emmanuel Mounier, "Christianity and the Idea of Progress," in *Be Not Afraid, op. cit.*, p. 70. Freire spoke with approval of these premises in *Education as the Practice of Freedom*, translated by Myra Ramos (New York: Seabury Press, 1973), p. 12.

23. See Peter L. Berger, "'Consciousness Raising' and the Vicissitudes of Policy," in *Pyramids of Sacrifice* (New York: Basic Books, 1975), pp. 111-132.

24. DeWitt, *op. cit.*, pp. 183-187.

25. Marx himself wrote about dependent and false consciousness. Sigmund Freud, Erich Fromm, Frantz Fanon and others have written about the social conditioning of the consciousness of the oppressed and its alienating effect. Regarding the contribution of Freud to Freire's thought, see Harriet Sherwin, "Paulo Freire, His Philosophy and Pedagogy of Teaching Reading" (unpublished [at this writing] monograph delivered at the Sixth World Congress on Reading in Singapore, Aug. 19, 1976), pp. 8f.

26. Paulo Freire, "The Educational Role of the Churches in Latin America," *art. cit.,* pp. 5-14.

27. Paulo Freire, "Conscientizing as a Way of Liberating," translation of a talk given in Rome in 1970 and published in the Latin American Documentation Series of the U.S. Catholic Conference (LADOC) *Keyhole Series* (Washington, D.C.: USCC Division for Latin America, 1973), Vol. I, p. 8.

The notes here and following Part II serve as a partial bibliography of Paulo Freire's works. Those readers who seek more complete information about his works are directed to the quotational bibliography prepared by Professor John Ohliger for the special occasional paper *Paulo Freire: A Revolutionary Dilemma for the Adult Educator,* edited by Stanley M. Grabowski (Syracuse University: Publications in Continuing Education and E.R.I.C. Clearinghouse on Adult Education, 1972). The Institute of Cultural Action (27, Chemin des Crets, 1218 Grand Saconnex, Geneva, Switzerland) furnishes information regarding publications by and about Paulo Freire that have appeared since 1972.

Part II
Philosophy

I

The summary of Paulo Freire's life and survey of some of the more important influences and themes shaping his thought lead us to a point where we can now take a closer look at his educational philosophy. One could easily be discouraged from attempting an analysis of Freire's philosophy by the nature of his writings. Is it not violence to try to impose a framework employing conventional divisions of educational philosophy (theories of reality, theories of knowledge, classification of values, and pedagogy) upon a dialectical investigation of culture and education? I think that it could be an act of violence if one made any claim that by *talking about* Freire's epistemology or axiology in a few pages he pretended to offer an exhaustive and definitive explanation of Freire's ideas. I make no such assertion, and by my attempt to state Freire's thought in several propositions I do not wish to convey the impression that one can reduce his writing to a few simple tenets.

All I attempt in the pages to follow is an introduction to some of the basic principles and premises upon which Freire's pedagogy is grounded. He nowhere separates any branch of philosophy from his pedagogical theory. I have chosen to speak of his theory of reality or theory of knowledge or axiology for the purpose of offering an *approach* to understanding his pedagogy. Nothing else is intended, and I am encouraged to think that Freire would not be offended by my approach. As we shall see, he has written that although it is impossible to dichotomize subjectivity from objectivity, or to separate human consciousness from the object of consciousness, it is nevertheless legitimate to talk about subjectivity or the object of consciousness in order to examine them. I want to answer the question "How does Freire think that people should educate themselves?" by answering three prior questions: "How does Freire define reality?" "How does Freire think that men and women can know reality?" and "What does Freire think is worthwhile?" Then I believe it will be possible to make some concluding remarks about his pedagogy and Freire's unique contributions to modern education.

II
"WHAT IS REAL?"

We have alluded to the dialectical nature of Freire's thought. Understanding reality involves knowing it, and one may say that the interaction of Freire's epistemology with his theory of reality is crucial, for dialectical understanding of man is found in understanding what man is *not*, and, more importantly, what man *is* as he exists in relationship with the world. For Freire, the world of other men and animals and plants and things does not exist without man the knower, who alone is capable of perception of reality and at the same time is also capable of perception. Man never exists apart from the world, and his relationship with the world is unique: a possibility of orientation to the world by an act of knowing, an orientation to the world through thought-language. As a result Freire does not

other, inseparable from their activity, undeciding, a-
mporal, determined by their species. Men are beings-
-themselves, reflective, determined but also deter-
ning, challenged, not merely stimulated, self-reflec-
e and capable of commitment to the project of his-
ical becoming.

4. *Some men only "live" and fail to "exist."* A
rollary to the statement that existence is a state of
ng that animals and some humans do not enjoy is
eire's illustration of the states of alienation of both the
pressors and of the oppressed. The oppressed, by
nial of their right to name the world, to direct their re-
ionship with the world, are denied the right to *have*
ich is a condition for all men to exist: they are re-
ced to a state of being-for-another. The oppressors on
other hand overlook the necessity of having as a
ndition for all men to exist and insist upon their
vilege to *have more* and thus cease to exist. They live
a dehumanized state, dehumanizing themselves and
people they oppress.

5. *Human existence is a task of praxis.* The ability
men to reflect upon reality as "not-I" and upon
mselves as "I," as subjects who can author and au-
nticate their relationships with the world, unveils
the man-world relationships and the subjects
mselves as unfinished tasks. Freire borrows the
ns "hominize" from Teilhard de Chardin and
axis" from Marx to describe the purpose of these
s: by combining reflective activity with his actions
gives human meaning to history and culture. If he
ents himself with mere reflections (only theorizing
ut his relationships with the world), he fails to hom-
 these relations because he limits himself to ver-
m. Alternatively he runs the risk of failing to re-

discuss the reality of man or of the world or even of
plants and animals without reference to the orientation
process of thought-language. One finds repeated references to "authentic" or "inauthentic" consciousness
and states of existence in which men are or are not
alienated according to their ability to utilize thought-
language in true praxis. Because of the centrality of the
process of orientation to reality through critical reflection and thought-language, a process of knowing and
naming in which subjectivity and objectivity are united,
Freire makes comments about what is real in the context of discussions of how humans know. How he goes
about this will be made clearer in the discussion of epistemology to follow. For the time being it is necessary to
bracket his theory of knowing and simply remark that
he proceeds to speak of what is "real" by defining what
is "unreal," what is "human" by what is "inhuman" or
"dehumanized," and what is "true" or "critically perceived" or "authentic" by mention of what is "false" or
"naively perceived" or "inauthentic."

1. *Reality is experenced by men[1] as a process.*
When studying reality men can fragment it, devoting
attention now at one time, now at another, to different
moments of the dialectical historical process. In doing
so they often commit the errors of mechanistic objectivism or solipsistic idealism, either reducing men and
the world to things or to abstractions, and so fail to discover reality as process. Men are situated in the spatio-
temporal conditions of history, conditions which are
perceived as contradictions which can keep men submerged. (For example, the "culture of silence" that
Freire describes is an example of such a contradiction.)
But men are not limited by contradiction; they possess
the ability to emerge and intervene in the historical pro-

cess, and, for Freire, emergence through transformation implies an ability of men "to be more" than they are when submerged in a situation of contradiction. They can emerge only insofar as they view reality as a totality and act through critical reflection to transform it.

2. *Men can never be understood apart from their relationship with the world through thought-language.* Reality is non-dualistic and implies constant interaction between man as a thinking subject and history and culture. Freire does not separate objectivity from subjectivity. Man is both a cause and an effect of history and culture, and when (as in a dependent culture) he is denied the opportunity to engage in authentic thought-language to transform history, he becomes alienated from reality. Alienation is due to the fact that his thought-language does not reflect reality as process, but expresses a distortion using thought-language to describe reality as if it were static. Freire speaks of thought-language as a unity mediating the world to man because thought is impossible without language, and both of them are impossible without the world to which they refer. Only men are capable of thought-language, and for Freire the "human word" or "naming reality" is not confined to formation of vocabulary. The "human word" is a combination of thought and action to humanize history and culture.[2]

3. *Men are different from animals.* Men and women are the only beings who have relationships with the world. They differ from animals who are a-historical, who live in an eternal today, who have a-critical contacts with the world, who are only in the world. Men are both in and with the world, differentiated from animals by a capacity to *reflect* (this includes the opera-

tions of intentionality, temporality, and tran
by which they become beings of relation, ar
pacity to *finalize* their relationships with the
like animals, the consciousness and actions
historical. Men dimensionalize their relatior
the world into epochs that indicate a *here* r
there, a *now* relative to a *past* and a *future*.
create history and are in turn created by histo

The capacity to finalize activity makes
of men fundamentally different from the acti
mals. Animals perform, acting according to
tions of men, so that their action really is tl
of men. Only men *work* because only men a
tentions. Similarly the capacity to reflect di
activities of men from animal actions becau
discover the contradictions of reality that del
it-situations"—i.e., only men discover t
presents itself as a problem to be transfo
men therefore are capable of praxis; only n
to create. Animals and men who are unat
their critical powers never achieve the rel
integration *with* the world; their state of b
in the world, accommodated to the world
Animals and men who do not separate the
their consciousness from their activities liv
of silence because they cannot name the w

Integration with the world is possible
that man utilizes his power to reflect not
actions but upon himself as the subject i
sion-making is seated, as the "I" of his
a world which is "not-I" but which can I
transformed by human designs and work
men are said to exist while animals merel

Animals are beings-in-themselves

flect when he acts, and this course of behavior is
dehumanized because it is only activism which ignores
the need to encounter and to respect other men and
women as beings-for-themselves. Neither verbalism nor
activism is real praxis which always combines reflection
with action to create the human world of ideas, symbols, language, science, religion, art, and production.
Freire holds that either operation—mere intellec-
tualizing or action for action's sake—is alienated and
alienating because each lacks human commitment and
makes dialogue impossible.

6. *Men, situated in history, are unfinished.* Our
first remark about Freire's view of reality observed that
men experience reality as a process. As reflective and
finalizing beings the reality they discover is seen to be
historical, and they themselves are revealed as historical beings with a past, present, and future. Men, too,
are process. Their praxis is a permanent task of becoming. Freire holds that as a historical and cultural being
man experiences himself situated in a condition that
implies he is a being who becomes:

> Man is man to the extent his condition of being
> expresses itself in these dialectical opposites: to be
> and to be-becoming. They characterize him as a
> historical and cultural being.[4]

"To be" and "to be-becoming" are the English equiva-
lent of Freire's words *ser y estar siendo* which express
man's mode of being and becoming as situated in spa-
tio-temporal reality.

7. *Man has a twofold ontological vocation: to become a subject and "to name the world."* Another
means Freire employs to speak of man as an unfinished

project of praxis is his often repeated statement that man has an ontological vocation to become more fully human. If men reflect on themselves they make three discoveries: (a) they are capable of reflecting upon their reflections, (b) they are in a situation (i.e., in history), and (c) they are becoming. These discoveries and the constant process of reflection on one's self and one's situatedness are operations proper to subjects. Animals and other objects do not reflect, so they do not discover themselves to be anything. But man's discovery of himself as a being-for-himself cannot be limited to one moment in history. Man has to re-create himself as a subject by continual reflection. Here the existentialist strain in Freire is borne out by his designation of man as a subject in process of becoming when he calls man a "creator and re-creator" and a "searcher." Men who fail to reflect or who cease to reflect and to search also cease existing and live unauthentically. Unauthentic living is also signified by action that treats other men as objects. Freire characterizes the task of becoming a subject as a vocation because men have to return daily to the task. He asserts that the indispensable means by which men become subjects who respect others' subjectivity is dialogical action, an activity which will receive separate treatment in Sections IV and V of this chapter.

As a subject, man is empowered to interact with the world. When subjectivity and objectivity are united through authentic actions transforming the world, man becomes the creator and author of history. Freire generally terms the transforming of cultural action of this nature as "naming the world." Drawing upon Western philosophical emphasis of *logos* (the word) and upon the Genesis myth in which Adam's dominion over the universe was signified by his activity of naming the animals, Freire says that men become fully human when they are capable of uttering their own *logos*, of speaking authentically as subjects. By uttering authentic words, man creates culture which in turn gives human meaning to history and thus "names" the world. Because Freire's philosophy is elaborated with reference to literacy campaigns, he frequently stresses the right of every man to be able to use (say, write, publish) his own word—*decir su propia palabra*—to emerge from the condition of literary and political marginality to relate with the world by naming it.

8. *Man-world relationships reveal reality as a problem: the thematic universe and limit situations.* Pictures of reality in philosophy, myth, propaganda or slogans which portray it as other than process are immobilizing, fixating forces. Historical man is not restricted to an eternal present and so experiences reality in each epoch as a problem to be solved. Past and present and future are not isolated but interconnected units providing continuity of history. Freire says that each epochal unit is characterized by its own themes:

An epoch is characterized by a complex of ideas, concepts, hopes, values, and challenges in dialectical interaction with their opposites, striving toward plenitude. The concrete representation of many of these ideas, values, concepts, and hopes, as well as the obstacles which impede man's full humanization, constitute the themes of that epoch. These themes imply others which are opposing or even antithetical; they also indicate tasks to be carried out and fulfilled.[5]

These themes, like the structures within which they emerge, overlap and interplay with their opposites throughout history. They constitute the "thematic universe" within which men live. When themes appear in dialectical contradiction to other themes, their antagonism causes men to take up contradictory positions, with some men defending themes that distort reality, while others embrace themes that unveil reality as a human task. The problematic aspect of reality is discovered in what Freire terms "limit situations":

> In the last analysis, the *themes* both contain and are contained in *limit-situations*; the *tasks* they imply require *limit-acts*. When the themes are concealed by the limit-situations and thus are not clearly perceived, the corresponding tasks—men's responses in the form of historical action—can be neither authentically nor critically fulfilled. In this situation, men are unable to transcend the limit-situations to discover that beyond these situations— and in contradiction to them—lies an *untested feasibility*.[6]

Themes are not things and do not exist outside men. They are discovered through investigation of men's thought. As that investigation gives rise to discovery of limit situations and the need for men to posit limit acts to humanize history and culture, reality is seen to be a challenge.

9. *To exist is to act politically for hominization.* The human world is revealed in a dialectical social structure, composed of an infrastructure which is the result of man's work and his relations with the world to give it meaning, and a political superstructure which

expresses the infrastructure. Interplay of permanence and change characterizes the social structure, but it is possible for men to act a-historically, trying to ignore the dialectic and allowing the superstructure to overdetermine the infrastructure. As an example of overdetermination Freire gives the efforts of elites who try to maintain a culture of silence. They introject myths into one or another political form, idealizing the superstructure as permanence to prevent social change.[7]

The only way for men to exist (to be "fully human") is to so act upon the world that the dialectic of permanence and change is preserved in the social structure. This implies the critical reflective process by which men overcome limit situations. Inevitably praxis involves political activity. Freire claims that at the beginning of his work with illiterates he did not foresee the extent of political entanglements stemming from his pedagogy, but in later works emphasis upon the non-neutrality of all education and insistence that true education must lead to revolutionary activity justify the assertion that for Freire "to exist is to take political action in favor of hominization."

III
"HOW CAN ONE KNOW REALITY?"

Our outline of Freire's theory of reality underscored the mediation of man-world relationships through thought-language. Just as man does not exist independently of the world, neither does thinking or knowing exist independently from the relationship man-world. Dialectical relations of men with the world exist independently of how they are perceived, but that does not mean these relations cannot be perceived at all. As a reflective being man is capable of considering reality as a whole, perhaps temporarily objectifying it in the sense that he focuses his attention on what is "not-I" to discover himself as an "I," as person and subject.

It is legitimate to speak of human thought and knowledge, of perception, of man's unique ability to perceive his perception. But Freire says that this cannot be done in such a way as to reify those operations, so objectifying them that they are understood to have existence apart from the relation man-world. It is because man is incomplete that he is able to treat himself, his thought, and his actions as objects of reflection. Indeed it is part of the task of becoming human that has been described above.

1. *Thinking and knowing are not independent of history and culture.* Thought-language mediates reality to men. There is no reality apart from history and human culture. Because reality is process, thinking and knowing are also unfinished. Thought-language is a process of creating knowledge which is what men use to create and re-create reality. Only conscious beings can think, and their consciousness is always consciousness-becoming. Thinking involves the process of discovering relationships previously unperceived in relation with the world. When authentic, it does not attempt to separate consciousness from the world because it does not dichotomize reflection and action.

Knowledge is a form of praxis, a process in which man begins to reflect on his orientation to the world by objectifying his actions, reflecting upon them in order to return to new action and reflection. Freire says that this dialectical process means "ad-miring" reality (the term is hyphenated here to emphasize its literal mean-

ing, *gazing at*), an operation in which man understands
what is real as a problem to be solved by his own actions. "Ad-miration" is also accompanied by "re-ad-
miration" (*gazing back at one's ad-miration*), another
moment of the knowing process in which man criticizes
his "ad-miration" of reality in order to overcome errors
in perception.[8] The two operations of "ad-miring" reality and "re-admiring" former "ad-mirations" are what
constitute critical knowing without which man cannot
act authentically. Freire says that one truly knows only
when he moves toward reflection and action upon the
world.

⊢ 2. *Subjectivity and objectivity are not dichotomized in a true act of knowing.* Freire speaks of
human knowing, of consciousness of reality, of "ad-
miration" and "re-ad-miration" of reality, but nearly
every use of these words or phrases is accompanied
with a caution that his language may be taken in two
different ways which seriously distort his thought. He
names the two epistemological errors: (a) subjective
idealism and (b) mechanistic objectivism. The first
error becomes possible if "ad-miration" and "re-ad-
miration" of human perception are understood to identify thought with the object of consciousness. This error
leads to solipsism. The mechanistic error arises when
one ignores the fact that human consciousness is also a
part of reality, falsely presuming that consciousness is
a copy of reality. Either error will lead men to act
uncritically, a-historically, and in an unauthentic fashion:

> In reality consciousness is not just a copy of the
> Real, nor is the Real only a capricious construc-
> tion of consciousness. It is only by way of an un-

derstanding of the dialectical unity, in which we find solidarity between subjectivity and objectivity, that we can get away from the subjectivist error as well as the mechanical error. And then we must take into account the role of consciousness or of the "conscious being" in the transformation of reality.

How can one explain, for example, in subjectivist terms, the position of human beings—as individuals, generation or social class—confronted with a given historic situation in which they "fit" independent of either their consciousness or their will? And how to explain, on the other hand, the same problem from a mechanical point of view? If consciousness arbitrarily creates reality, a generation or social class could, rejecting the given situation in which they live, transform it by a simple relevant gesture. Likewise, if consciousness were only a simple reflection of reality, a given situation would be eternally the given situation. Reality would be the determinant "subject" in itself.

Human beings would be only yielding objects. In other words, the given situation would change of itself. That means seeing History as a mythical entity, outside of and superior to human beings, able to capriciously command them from above and beyond.[9]

If one keeps this double admonition against subjective idealism and mechanistic objectivism in mind, he can examine Freire's references to acts of knowing, to subjectivity, and to objectivity, always understanding that

Freire only separates subjectivity from objectivity in order to talk about them. He never intends to speak of man apart from the object of his consciousness or of a world apart from human consciousness. Without man to name it, the world does not exist. At the same time, contrary to the assertion of those who call Freire an idealist, consciousness does not precede the world (determining it from outside), nor does consciousness follow the world as a product (completely determined by it).[10]

Freire does not discuss the two epistemological errors for the sake of idle speculation or to add academic trimmings to his pedagogy. It is rather the political nature of his pedagogy that demands he steer a course between objectivity and subjectivity. The objectivist and subjectivist errors both have political and pedagogical ramifications. In the political sphere Freire says that they lead men into the sectarianism practiced by the Right (who treat men as objects) as well as by the Left (who try to predetermine history by expecting the future to change when men change their consciousness). Sectarians of the Right and Left both act a-historically, the former by trying to domesticate history so that the future will duplicate the present, the latter by rashly presuming that history will assume a configuration determined a priori by human consciousness.[11] In either case the sectarian fails to think dialectically and overlooks the transforming role of human reflection and action.

The influence upon pedagogy that Freire attributes to these epistemological errors is discussed more completely in the pages ahead. At this point it should suffice to point out that Freire's statement that subjectivity and objectivity are not capable of being dichotomized asserts simultaneously that (a) there is such a thing as material reality and that (b) human consciousness has a role to play in re-creating it. Denying objectivity to man denies the possibility of action; denying subjectivity denies that man is a person who can author history. Subjectivism makes men immobile while objectivism makes them dehumanized.

/ 3. *Oppressed states of consciousness constitute an historical epistemological problem.* How men know depends upon the manner in which they experience reality mediated by thought-language. Reflection upon reality discovers an historical situation of violence in which some men perpetuate personal privileges by maintaining others in a state of oppression. Exploitation implies two different manners of viewing the world and of behavior toward other men. For the oppressors, defined by Freire as those who initiate violence, the right to have more is their exclusive right. Other men are not beings-for-themselves but only beings-for-others. The exploited, passive recipients of violence, therefore, view the world and other men in a fashion prescribed for them in large part by their oppressors. Freire says that oppressed consciousness is afflicted with "duality" in viewing the world, itself, and other men. On the one hand, education and methods of government that extend oppression force the oppressed to view themselves and other men as their oppressors want them to view reality. At the same time, no matter how dehumanized their state and in spite of historical treatment as objects, the oppressed are human beings—always capable of becoming subjects. Freire says that the oppressed "house" the oppressor within their consciousness, but the situation is not a natural state. It is an alienated state resulting from violence and interfering with man's ontological vocation to become more fully human.

Freire borrows two terms from Erich Fromm to contrast oppressor consciousness with the state of consciousness that allows for a true act of knowing. Oppressor consciousness is "necrophilic" because it seeks to dehumanize others while dehumanizing the oppressors. This is perverted love, sadism which by loving dehumanization loves death. Men who know humanly are characterized by "biophilic" consciousness, loving themselves and others and thereby loving life.

4. *As man emerges from the duality of oppressed consciousness, his consciousness develops from "magical" consciousness to "critical" consciousness.* The oppressed and oppressing consciousnesses of which Freire speaks indicate two overdetermined alienated states of the oppressor-oppressed contradiction. But by no means do they exhaust the states of human consciousness about which Freire speaks. As man moves from a state of alienation to hominization he does not progress immediately but by stages. He is not oppressed one day and liberated the next. Since human consciousness is conditioned by reality as experienced and mediated through thought-language, Freire employs an analogy from grammar (transitivity) to describe states of human consciousness.

In closed and oppressive societies such as that experienced by peasants, human consciousness is "intransitive." Men live immersed in agrarian interests, experiencing reality very much as animals do. Intransitive consciousness is narrow in interest, uninvolved with existence as a problem. It is characterized by a fatalistic, magical attitude that attributes facts and historical circumstances to superior powers. These may be designated "Fortune" or "God" or "gods" or perhaps identified exclusively with the few men who possess political power, land, wealth, and armed might. Intransitive consciousness does not question the powers; it merely assumes that they are given determinants of the historical situation. Men who think intransitively may try to assuage or please these powers by religious or magical rites. If the rites fail to produce the desired effect and a crop is destroyed or a harvest is meager, the human situation is not considered a problem in which men can intervene, but rather "Destiny" or "God's will." Magical thinking is typical of oppressed consciousness in its most extreme form.

"Transitive" consciousness comes about when men begin to experience reality as a problem. Through intentionality men can grow as their interests and preoccupations reach out to other spheres and begin to dialogue with other men, with the world, and with its Creator. Freire, however, maintains that in its first stages transitive consciousness is only "semi-intransitive" and "naive" at a later stage, seeking simple explanations which are little more than magical solutions. Freire calls the first stage of emergent consciousness "semi-intransitive" because it does not yet know reality in a true act of knowing; it is still "quasi-immersed."[12]

The second stage of transitive consciousness is naive transitive consciousness. In *Education as the Practice of Freedom* Freire spoke of twentieth-century Brazilian society as "semi-intransitive" and "naively intransitive" because it was in a state of transition away from the consciousness of a closed society. Nevertheless it remained an oppressed consciousness and susceptible to the danger that Freire sees as inherent in all populist movements: manipulation. Power elites can manipulate the oppressed either by force, or else by propaganda, slogans, or dehumanizing utilization of technology. Because semi-intransitive and naive transitive consciousness seek simple solutions and presume that they are superior to facts and to history, they readily accept manipulative myths formulated by elites to maintain oppression.

Therefore, in its first stages transitive consciousness is in danger of distortion in two ways. First, the oppressors living in a traditional society become aware that those upon whom they depend may endanger the oppressors' hitherto unrestricted freedoms. They respond to the challenge by seeking new means (appeal to patriotism, fear of communism, invocation of religious myths to canonize ecclesiastical and secular authority, etc.) to manipulate popular consciousness. In the second instance the oppressed accept the solutions of elites and live according to myths and educational practices prescribed for them by the powerful. They become massified, perhaps modernized, but they do not develop. In each case transitivity of the oppressor and of the oppressed is distorted into irrationality.

True knowing is possible when men can attain a state of "critical transitivity." This state of consciousness is one in which men think as subjects. The critically conscious human being does not reach out for simple solutions (running the risk of dehumanizing himself). Naive transitive consciousness permits men to adapt to the world; critical consciousness allows them to integrate themselves with the world through cultural action. Critical consciousness implies apprehension and analysis of the causal relationships in which man discovers himself "to be in a situation." Apprehension and analysis ought to present reality as problem and challenge. They make possible an open society.

Freire's analogy of transitivity embodied by different states of human consciousness asserts that men's actions depend upon their comprehension of reality. Every act of comprehension conditions every action of response. If men have a magical consciousness they act magically and fail to emerge from oppression. If their understanding is naive, their actions are easily reduced to irrationality. If their understanding of reality is a critical perception of reality, their response can be transitive, a combination of reflection and action in authentic praxis.

5. *Critical consciousness is intentionality.* Edmund Husserl parted company with Kant and the British empiricists with his assertion that consciousness can know the structure of real things because the nature of consciousness is what he called "intentionality." How he modified the concept of intentionality originally learned from his teacher Franz von Brentano need not concern us here. It is enough to recall that Husserl's phenomenology maintained a certain realism:

> The science of phenomena therefore is the science of things that appear, as they appear. The notion of appearance does not imply an obstacle that somehow limits our knowing, a barrier that must be overcome if truth and reality are to be obtained. Rather, there is truth in the appearances of things, and things are to be taken as they appear, no more and no less.[13]

Freire borrows the notion of consciousness as intentionality from Husserl and states that the critical consciousness of subjects is consciousness become intentionality. By this he means that the consciousness of subjects is active: reality does not enter consciousness to fill it; it is the other way around. Consciousness goes out to reality, examining it, exploring it, questioning it.

When men perceive all the causal relationships of a situation, including their own power to reflect and intervene in history, Freire says that they are "fully intent" upon the universe because they thereby discover what was already implicit but inconspicuous in the phenomena they perceive.[14] The way of knowing that discovers the subjective role of human consciousness, "intending" the universe, affects Freire's pedagogical theory because it means that all acts of knowing which objectify the universe and man himself do not treat the world or man in a neutral fashion and reduce man to a mere spectator. In human knowing—intentionality—every objectification, every act of abstraction is performed so that knowledge appears as a challenge to man. What he comes to know abstractly must be given meaning by his activity.

6. *Knowing is a social activity.* Since man exists in a world populated by other men, his discovery of himself as subject implies his discovery of others' subjectivity. Dehumanized knowing implies treating other men as objects. Humanistic acts of knowing imply communication through dialogue with others to determine how they experience reality so that men can act upon history together:

> To know, which is always a process, implies a dialogical situation. There is not, strictly speaking, "I think," but "we think." It is not "I think" which constitutes "we think," but, on the contrary, it is "we think" that makes it possible for me to think.[15]

That knowing which fails to reflect upon the reality lived by other men is artificial. Even when pursued in the interests of scientific detachment, objectivity in knowing is incomplete when anti-dialogical, because it is inhuman. Hence the statement above that for Freire "critical consciousness is intentionality" should be understood to include the social dimension of authentic knowing: "Critical consciousness is co-intentionality."

7. *Critical transitive consciousness is achieved through a permanent process called conscientization.* Freire's ontology asserts that men exist when they act politically. One of the introductory remarks in *Pedagogy of the Oppressed* observes that dehumanization through denial of political freedom is not just an ontological possibility but a tragic historical reality.[16] The path away from dehumanized living to the ontological possibility of participation in the political process is made passable by involvement of human consciousness in the process that Freire calls *conscientization*. It is another way of describing the role of consciousness in human praxis. Freire has pointed out that by concentrating on the role of consciousness in the process of liberation, he follows Marx and Engels who observed that freedom from oppression is facilitated by making oppression "more oppressive" when men realize (are conscious of) their oppression.[17] The term *conscientization* did not originate with Freire, but was used by a member of one of the teams he worked with in Brazil. Freire realized the special suitability of the word for expressing his pedagogical theory, and began to incorporate it in his writing and lectures. He says it was really Dom Helder Camara who publicized the word in Europe and in the United States.[18]

Conscientization is a basic dimension of human reflective action which expresses the knowing process whereby oppressed individuals and classes become subjects. Even though human consciousness may be conditioned, because it is *human* it can recognize that it is conditioned.[19] In its spontaneous activity the oppressed consciousness' fundamental position toward the world is magical or naive. Deepened consciousness of the man-world situation makes men aware of their state of oppression, but this is not conscientization. It is only a first step toward conscientization, awareness of being-in-a-situation which Freire says is the *prise de conscience* described by Gabriel Marcel.[20] It is true that the *prise de conscience* signifies supplanting a naive perception of reality with a critical perception, but is not enough to achieve human liberation. Liberation comes about through conscientization when men "take possession" of reality by demythologizing it and acting upon it.[21] As praxis it is an unfinished process because discovering a new reality by critical transitivity does not exhaust conscientization. The new reality must become the object of a new reflection since what is authentic in one historical epoch will not necessarily be authentic in another.[22] Finally, since knowledge is social, conscientization is not limited to the individual: discovery of the individual's oppression should lead to discovery of the oppressed as a class.[23] Class consciousness of oppression leads men to apprehend historical reality as susceptible of transformation. The more men are conscientized the more they exist. Freire compares the entire process of conscientization to a "painful birth" or an "Easter experience" in which human consciousness of the oppressor and the oppressed dies in order to be reborn.[24]

8. *"To know" is to act politically for hominization: "to know" is "to exist."* By now the interdependence of Freire's theory of reality with his epistemology is evident. Men exist authentically when they can name

the world, giving meaning to history and culture, they can only name it when they know it authentically. A consciousness fully intent upon the world is consciousness that seeks to combine reflection with action for human liberation. Due to the historical situation of oppression, consciousness has to struggle to emerge through a process (conscientization) that utilizes dialogue and communication. But Freire denies that it is enough to transform consciousness to achieve liberation. (In fact he denies he ever said that, although some continue to accuse him of that idealist error.)[25] Change of consciousness must be accompanied by actions for liberation which are ultimately political. Hence conscientization, necessary for true acts of knowing, has a political dimension. For Freire "to know" is "to exist."

IV
"WHAT SHOULD BE PRIZED?"

The statements about knowing and reality above have in many ways anticipated Freire's reply to the axiological question "What is worthwhile?" What is valuable to men is their humanity and their ontological vocation to become fully human. In dialectical thinking values are suggested by the historical contradictions which impede the process of becoming fully human. Alienation suggests its opposite challenge: hominization. The human thematic universe in which Freire ascertains the fundamental generative theme of the modern epoch to be oppression suggests its opposite theme, liberation, as the supreme human value. Therefore all the remarks which follow on this and subsequent pages are simply elaboration of what is implied in man's vocation to be more fully human and to know in a true act of knowing.

1. *The supreme human goal is humanization through a process of liberation.* Freire states explicitly: "This is the principal finality of human existence: to become human."[26] Because man is man and not animal this process is possible only when men are integrated with the world. However, man has a problem: as he experiences history he finds that the indispensable condition for human completion, human freedom, is not attained. Man is only in a process of evolution which in the present era reveals that the majority of mankind is alienated.

The central problem in becoming fully human is the problem of liberation from this animal-like state. Human liberation, hominization, involves a struggle dependent upon emergent consciousness and the praxis that should result from heightened consciousness. Freire stresses the idea that liberation is not a terminal static state but a continuous and permanent transformation of reality in favor of the liberation of man. What emerges in the process of transformation is a new man in process of liberation. (Freire is in familiar company here; we have heard a great deal about the New Man from Marx and Mao, not to mention Paul of Tarsus some nineteen centuries before them!)

Humanization on Freire's terms is not pursuit of individual liberation. The goal of humanization is a social goal, and man's need to be a being-for-himself is attained when a society is able to become a being-for-itself. Individual men neither know nor exist outside of society. The fellowship and solidarity that Freire demands in the task of human liberation therefore identifies liberation as the most important task and value of the human race.

2. *Authentic praxis seeks permanent transformation of the social structure.* This statement is a corollary to the first, expressing the sociopolitical dimensions of humanization. Freire says that human social structure is not all permanence nor is it all change, but rather "duration" of the contradiction permanence-change. "Duration" is a concept he borrows from Henri Bergson, intended to illustrate life neither as purely static nor as constant change isolated from previous determinations made by human work. The social structure is renewed through change of its economic, political, social, and cultural institutions which do not appear out of nothing. They are products of man's former creative actions. When the institutions become old, some men refuse to change them, attempting to make them permanent. Others opt for change so that men become divided into progressives and reactionaries. Explaining the social structure as "duration" asserts that what is permanent is not a given superstructure, but process: change arises from the re-creation of previous actions.[27]

It is difficult to discuss finality in Freire's thought without observing that the goals sought in the process of humanization are not goals in themselves but really values which suggest and point to higher goals. Therefore I would like to borrow a term coined by the American Reconstructionist Theodore Brameld to speak of social goals—"value-means." In response to the question "What is worthwhile?" one may list from Freire's philosophy the following: cultural action for freedom, conscientization,[28] politicization, radicalization, and finally political and cultural revolution. Each action as a step toward humanization is a value, but none of these values is an end in itself. They are all means to attain the highest human value, permanent emergence of the new man in a socio-political structure that guarantees every person the right to participate in the process of liberation.

Freire is insistent that participation of all men, even from the very first moments of their liberation, be clearly designated as a goal to be kept in mind at every stage by the leaders and the masses. Populism is certainly a value for Freire, but nearly every mention of populism is coupled with words of caution to the effect that populist movements are easily manipulated, achieving only a massification of men in which they remain alienated.

Freire is critical of all populist movements and revolutions (such as those of Mexico, Soviet Russia, East Germany) which deny the oppressed the right to participate in their liberation. He is realistic enough to say that revolutionary leaders cannot hand freedom to the masses, nor can they legitimately use methods of oppressors on a "temporary" basis to free others at a post-revolutionary date. Leaders may bear responsibility for coordination of revolutionary effort, but Freire maintains they invalidate their own praxis when they deny authentic praxis to the oppressed in the name of liberation.[29]

How far is the radical transformation of human social structure to proceed? Freire never seems to go beyond admission of fondness for the revolutions of Mao Tse-tung in China and Fidel Castro in Cuba, and the assertion that liberation is not a terminal stage of conscientization, but a permanent process. Certainly his writings call for transformation of capitalist bourgeois society by throwing it out altogether.[30]

3. *Dialogue is the value-means indispensable for praxis.* Justification for the statement that Freire's educational philosophy is humanistic is probably nowhere so eloquently exemplified and substantiated as in his writings typifying cultural action as essentially dialogical. The role of dialogue in teaching, in learning, in politics, is a theme begun in *Education as the Practice of Freedom,* greatly expanded in the essays of *Sobre la Acción Cultural,* and the topic to which the entire final chapter of *Pedagogy of the Oppressed* is dedicated. His descriptions of dialogue at times are coldly philosophical (stressing it as a condition for men to become subjects), while at other times his praise of dialogue is lyrical, almost visionary, as he insists upon attitudes of trust, faith, humility, willingness to risk, and love without which dialogue is not possible.

Dialogue suitable for cultural action is not a simple exchange of views. Freire notes that Socratic dialogue exemplified in Plato's thought is not the kind of dialogue by which men engage in cultural action. Plato and Socrates used dialogue as a propaedeutic by which men were lead to rediscover ideas long forgotten. *Logos* (the pure world of reason) existed apart from man and was "seen" by men as they moved through dialogue away from sensation and opinion. In contrast Freire's dialogue is reflection upon man-world relationships, and has as its starting point the discovery of man existing in and with the world.[31] Freire rejects the exchange of viewpoints embodied in what he calls the "tactics of the Right." Neither oppressors nor would-be revolutionaries who utilize the tactics of the Right engage in dialogue because they speak to others in order to prescribe, to impose ideas upon them. The tactics are slogans, manipulations (among which Freire includes human relations techniques), and propaganda in the form of anti-dialogical "communiques" which may convey messages but do not communicate.[32]

Men only communicate, as Freire uses the word, when they relate with other men as subjects. Intersubjectivity is a relationship of "I-Thou" in which men respect one another and communicate in an atmosphere of sympathy with the ideas of other subjects. *¿Extensión o Communicación?* is a work entirely devoted to illustrating the impossibility of cultural action without communication. Dependent upon the social nature of knowing, men do not think without dialogue and they cannot engage in legitimate praxis without true knowing and thinking. Praxis must be dialogical to be true.

Freire's esteem of communication and disdain for communiques is exemplified by the affective posture he says denotes authentic dialogue. He first demands that men who dialogue must be loving. The object of love is other men and the world; men must love themselves, life, and other men. Love is characterized by commitment to other men and to the world, and commitment is evidenced by trust and faith in man's ability to create and direct distory. Dialogue requires that men be humble as they seek to know together, because dialogue is threatened and rendered impossible when one man assumes others are absolutely ignorant or jeopardizes dialogue by failing to perceive his own ignorance and need to seek knowledge in company with others. Freire is aware of the high-sounding rhetorical nature of words such as *love, trust, commitment, faith, communion, solidarity*, and even *dialogue*. At the same time he is impelled by a need for consistency with his epistemology which describes knowledge as social, ultimately dependent upon intersubjectivity.

This does not mean Freire's advocacy of love and dialogue as value-means obscures his revolutionary intentions. He underscores the notion that all attributes of cultural action demand risk. He is also aware that one cannot blindly trust every man's ability to dialogue because human consciousness houses the oppressor and is ambiguous. On this point Freire stumbles again, maintaining that mistrust of others by a revolutionary leader is only "being a realist" and he quotes Che Guevara to that effect.[33]

He is on firmer ground when he says that advocacy of open dialogical action is not advocacy of license. On the contrary he believes it defends real authority in the name of human freedom. In a state of oppression authoritarianism conflicts with freedom because authority is imposed. License would conflict similarly with freedom because it is anti-dialogical. When, however, authority is delegated (not imposed or merely transferred from one power bloc to another), Freire holds that authority makes freedom possible because authority delegated by the people is freedom-become-authority. [34]

4. *Authentic praxis implies commitment to Utopia.* Freire deliberately calls his thought and pedagogy *utopian.* They are a call for "prophetic" cultural action which engages in the prophet's two-fold project of "denunciation" and "annunciation." It is insufficient for men merely to possess a biophilic attitude; their knowledge of the ontological vocation to become more fully human should be completed by commitment to the vision of a better man-world relationship through cultural action. Utopian thought as defined by Freire is not idealism or advocacy of impracticality. It is orientation

and commitment to the future. If men engage in praxis they "denounce" what they discover to be dehumanizing and "announce" something better: a more fully human society. In a dehumanized state consciousness is conditioned by ideological myths, so a task of denunciation is the philosophical step of praxis subsequent to discovery of the alienating effect of ideology: demythologization. Subsequently the utopian is asked to replace political, economic, and religious myths by science. True science does not mythify technique or substitute modernization for development. It must take reflection upon the man-world relationship as its starting point, and respond to that reality critically, attempting to transform it without subordination to ideologies that seek to maintain the status quo.[35]

The union of science and philosophy achieved in authentic praxis is what Freire calls scientific humanism. His humanism is not the humanism traditionally espoused in Western culture which centers itself upon study of the past. Study of human letters which does not liberate is what he calls false humanism. Cultural action for freedom is humanistic employment of science and philosophy to humanize the universe. In a footnote to a chapter dealing with the problem of how expert knowledge is to be utilized for liberation, Freire explains his view of humanism:

By humanism the author does not understand, in this or in his other writings, the fine arts, classical aristocratic formation, or erudition. Nor does he understand it as an abstract ideal of a good man. True humanism is radical involvement with man-in-the-concrete. It is involvement which is directed toward the transformation of whatever objective

situation in which man-in-the-concrete is prohibit-
ed from being more.[36]

To avoid cultural action for domestication, men must
be committed to a new, utopian, reality.

  5. *Education as value-means should be cultural action for freedom and cultural revolution.* Freire says it
is unlikely that the oppressed can seek their own liberation without assistance from leaders who can initiate
the process. This necessitates clarity in objectives on the
part of leaders of liberation movements. If leaders intend dialogical humanization as an end they must also
intend the educational value-means to achieve it. The
education Freire prizes is two distinct moments of liberation: cultural action for freedom and cultural revolution. The first value-means to be sought by leaders of
the revolution is consciousness-raising praxis. Once
power is taken, the process should be prolonged in its
second moment, permanent cultural revolution.[37]

  Within a few paragraphs we will dwell at greater
length on Freire's educational theory. The purpose of
saying here that cultural action for freedom and cultural revolution are among the value-means of his philosophy is to underscore the importance Freire attributes
to education (defined according to his notion of humanism) in the process of liberation. Although Freire rarely
speaks of schools or school systems, he is far from
being a deschooler along the lines of the criticism of
Ivan Illich or Everett Reimer. It seems to me that the
overwhelming emphasis in Freire's books is upon education as the most important means (hence a principal
value) for achieving societal changes.

  6. *Religion is a value-means.* Freire is a thinker of
the Catholic Left. As a believing Catholic he accepts

some idea of creation of the universe and the presence of God in human history. As a spokesman for the Left he points out that to be a Christian does not necessarily mean one must be a reactionary and that to be a Marxist does not necessarily mean being a member of a dehumanizing bureaucracy.[38] Christians cannot remain passive in the face of oppression. Where (as in Latin America) Christian churches have served as instruments of alienation their practice of religion has been false. Christians should reject the order of exploitation and Freire is convinced that a scientific transformation of history is consonant with the teaching of the New Testament.[39] Religion is not a task for missionaries from First World countries to export to the Third World; an authentic Christian perspective considers all lands mission lands where the practice of religion should be part of the act of liberation.[40]

Christians who wish to continue educational work must realize they cannot be neutral. Among modern Christians Freire finds two groups: the "innocent" and the "astute." The innocent are those who believe social structures will change if the churches preach a change of heart. This is the error of subjective idealism that believes change of consciousness can effect social reality. The astute are those Christians who perceive the non-neutrality of education and then choose to engage in education either as cultural action for domination or for liberation.[41] Freire dismisses the churches' traditional works in education with the judgment that they have been domesticating. Churches that modernize their efforts by adapting techniques to pedagogy have little effect because they employ half-way measures. Authentic Christian education must be utopian and prophetic, utilizing the new awareness social sciences bring to theology to denounce dehumanized structures and announce a new order.[42]

When he speaks of Christianity, Freire again applies the metaphor of "speaking one's word." The Christian doctrine of the incarnation holds that Jesus is the "Word of God" and has been preached as a permanent presence of God in history that renders man helpless, eternally dependent upon a "will of God" which forbids man a role in determining his own history. Freire says this distorts the message preached by Jesus and limits men to a weak role of passive recipients of revelation. God's speaking of "His Word" should not keep man in a state of silence.

Freire contends that if the Christian revelation is as it claims to be, a saving message, it must be liberating in the sense it enables men to become subjects of their salvation and liberation. There is a legitimate role to be played by theology in this process of becoming a subject:

> Theological education ought not be more than a form of cultural action for liberation by means of which men replace their naive understanding of God—in so far as it is myth through which they become alienated—by another understanding: that in which God, as a presence in history nevertheless does not hinder men from "making history": the history of their liberation.[43]

A saying repeated in many of his works is that the process of becoming a subject involves an "Easter experience." In the case of the educator it means dying as the unilateral educator of the educatees.[44] In the case of anyone from the first world who presumes to teach or proselytize among peoples of the third world, it involves "dying" as a member of the first world in order to be "born again" in solidarity with the peoples of the third world. The "Easter experience" is one he insists upon for revolutionaries, missionaries, and pedagogues, and the metaphor is not used exclusively of religious values in his writings. The "Easter experience" is a precondition of authentic praxis.

V

FREIRE'S PROBLEM-POSING PEDAGOGY

We have mentioned that education is the most important value-means for the process of human liberation envisioned by Freire. Because Freire himself in *Education as the Practice of Freedom* and several other authors[45] have provided excellent illustrations in English of how his methodology was implemented in adult literacy programs, a recapitulation of method will not be repeated here. I am more concerned with relating his philosophy to general educational theory. Freire makes the claim that his educational theory is not limited to problems of adult education. He holds that his scientific revolutionary humanism is applicable (but never uniformly so) to every attempt to educate human beings. Let us see what he suggests for the content of education and what reforms are required by conscientization.

1. *The two stages of liberation have a fundamental educational quality.* Freire's ontology and epistemology assert that the relationship man-world is mediated by thought-language. Since thought-language is alienated by the historical situation of oppression, the relationship man-world is likewise alienated and oppressed.

All movement away from oppressed consciousness and alienated living in the world must therefore concern itself with authentic human expression so that thought and actions (in Freire's metaphor, man's "word," his "naming the world") will be authentic.[46]

Ability to move away from oppressed consciousness and alienated living requires political power. That power is found in most instances to be in the possession of those Freire names oppressors. Work on the part of the oppressed aimed at resolving the contradiction is cultural action, consciousness-raising education that is authentic in so far as it is utopian and corresponds to the human mode of being which is historical.[47] While the oppressed lack political power their educational activity cannot be systematic, so Freire discusses two stages implied by authentic education: (1) educational projects carried on, by, and with the oppressed before they take power, and (2) systematic education in the form of permanent cultural revolution. In each stage education, like historical social structures, is a process characterized by duration; it is a process which "is becoming and is not finished."[48] A historical mode of learning must address the fact that cultures of silence exist, and so the first stage of education may involve forms of cultural action that supply access to minimal, basic rights such as literacy. In the permanent stage of cultural revolution educational efforts can expand to embrace all fields of human knowledge which provide man with the skills necessary for making and re-making culture. As long as either stage sincerely seeks the permanent liberation of humanity, Freire considers it "humanist" education. "Humanitarian" education, carried on by oppressors to maintain the status quo, or pretended "revolutionary" activity that denies the peoples' right to participate in their education is <u>inauthentic cultural action</u>.

2. *Authentic pedagogy is undeniably political cultural action.* By repeatedly showing there is "no such thing as neutral education" Freire does not mean to imply (as many critics think he does) that his radical consciousness-raising educational theory pretends to a neutrality other pedagogies do not possess. Conscientization is not a purely mental process that simply makes men aware of their situation in history, for simple awareness without action leaves political structures untouched. Freire's exposition of educational theory suggests that men through dialogical education become co-authors of history. His writings are filled with criticisms of traditional banking and extension education methods used to preserve privilege or (worse still) imposed by revolutionaries to coerce people into believing their leadership is correct. When he says "there is no such thing as neutral education" all Freire is saying is that sectarians of the Right or of the Left often pretend they are neutral when they actually employ pedagogies of domestication. Authentic pedagogy is partial too, but it is partial in favor of humanization.[49]

3. *Traditional education employs "banking" methods.* Freire directs his criticism at the separation of teaching from learning. When teaching becomes entirely the activity of the one who instructs, and learning the "duty" of the student, the teacher is viewed as possessing knowledge as one might possess private property. Students are assumed to possess no knowledge and to be in need of receiving knowledge. Freire calls these attitudes and methods banking education because they reduce teaching to an activity of depositing bits of information and skills into a presumably empty and pas-

sive student mind. Banking education is used to domesticate men because it emphasizes transfer of existing knowledge to passive objects who memorize, recite, catalogue, and pay back according to schedule the bits of information deposited in their consciousness. By regarding knowledge as private property, banking educators are paternalists who view other men as objects of generosity, recipients of their "prescriptions" (because knowledge is a medicine to cure the illness of ignorance). As long as students are considered to be beings-for-others, education will continue to adapt them to oppression by indoctrinating methods.[50]

Freire calls banking education a type of violence. Banking educators mythify reality in an effort to submerge the creative consciousness of the students. They impose curricula, ideas, and values. When education takes the form of foreign or domestic aid it assumes a mechanicist position with regard to other men, reducing them to producers to be (a) "filled up" with skills or (b) trained as leaders to perpetuate alienation.[51]

Banking educational methods are erroneous because in dichotomizing teacher from student, they also dichotomize man from the world, believing that reality enters consciousness. As we saw above, this is a negation of Freire's idea of consciousness as co-intentionality. The consciousness of subjects is not empty, to be filled by transfer of information or skills in an act of knowing. As reflective subjects humans are curious and critical, seeking causal relationships in their perception of the world and of consciousness itself. As social beings they discover their thinking is checked and stimulated by the thinking and perception of other subjects. Emphasis upon transfer of information is unconcerned with communication or with intersubjectivity or with man's mode of knowing as co-intentionality. When communication is ignored only a partial view of reality can be presented.

Freire's impatience with banking education comes from recognition of its fragmentation of consciousness. Men need alternatives to traditional education because they are reflective beings. He claims the starting point of a humanizing education must be the resolution of the teacher-student contradiction.[52] Any other approach denies the creative aspect of the act of knowing and perpetuates oppression. The reflective nature of critical consciousness means that teachers and learners must seek to know together in order to transform the world. When they view knowing as social process the dichotomy can be resolved in the synthesis which emerges as "educators" become "educatees" and "educatees" become "educators."

4. *Dialogical education is problem-posing.* The alternative to banking education is educational theory and methodology which responds to man's vocation to be a subject. In as much as man is discovered in history to be denied realization of his subjectivity, educational content should correspond to the problems of emergent consciousness. This can occur when education is "philosophic anthropology," when educators perceive the central importance of the philosophical concept of consciousness and the anthropological concept of culture.[53] Education can take consciousness as a starting point, performing what Freire calls an "archaeology of the consciousness," an examination of the people's thinking which discovers superstitious, naive, and critical states of consciousness.[54] This examination does not study man or consciousness as things but rather asks, "What do men think?" "How do they think?" "What is their

vision of the world?" As the investigation continues, Freire stresses the role thinking plays in the making and remaking of the world. The investigation invites consciousness to assume an active attitude toward the world, discovering how history and culture are conditioned by ideas, beliefs, myths, art, science, manners, tastes, and political preferences. Human institutions and social structures turn back to act upon consciousness and their conditioning effect is either oppressing or liberating. What Freire hopes to achieve by his "archaeology of the consciousness" is discovery of history and culture (especially as embodied and acting upon men in their institutions and social structures) as the work of men, as problems to be solved by authentic praxis. Freire says this is discovery of the world as "giving" rather than "given."[55]

How does one go about investigating the people's thinking? By study of the thematic universe, the generative themes it suggests, and the tasks they in turn suggest for cultural action. If consciousness is shaped by newspapers and government propaganda, Freire suggests study of themes such as underdevelopment, hunger, dependence, the culture of silence, or the tactics of anti-dialogical education. These themes suggest other and opposite themes leading to discovery of limit situations and (one hopes) limit acts to liberate mankind.

Once literacy is achieved the task of education is still one of problematizing reality so that students become politically literate. Whatever the academic subject investigated (and Freire is aware that every discipline does not lend itself equally to the task), education should seek to problematize culture. In the hope of providing a summary statement of Freire's ped-

agogy the following schema is submitted as a general
outline of the three phases common to pre-literacy and
post-literacy education:

(1) INVESTIGATION   examination and discovery of human conscious-
ness as naive, supersti-
tious, critical.

(2) THEMATIZATION   (a) examination of the
thematic universe by re-
duction, coding, decodification;
(b) discovery of new gen-
erative themes suggested
by earlier themes

(3) PROBLEMATIZATION (a) discovery of limit situations and
(b) their corresponding
limit acts

leading to
AUTHENTIC PRAXIS:
permanent cultural action for liberation

The terms "reduction," "coding," "decodification," all
indicate steps Freire utilized in literacy programs to
present and represent the people's thinking by pictures,
slides, tape recordings, and discussions revealing the activity of humans as agents of culture, members of
agrarian or urban society, authors of foklore, etc. The
purpose of these presentations was to allow codification
of culture in highly meaningful generative words suit-

able for (1) teaching people to read while (2) suggesting generative themes that illustrate the role of consciousness in history and culture. His emphasis is as important to post-literacy phases of education as it is to the prior phase. Examples of reduction, codification, and decodification differ as subject matter differs in post-literacy phases. They are retained in the present schema to indicate that Freire would not omit study of consciousness or culture from *any* education, including even the study of physical sciences which he singles out for their non-neutral cultural properties.[56]

5. *Teachers and expert knowledge are not excluded from dialogical education.* Freire's opposition to banking education does not eliminate the role of teachers nor does it deny the legitimacy or necessity of expert knowledge. The attack upon traditional education does mean that roles of the educator and experts are different in education for liberation. Banking educators have absolutized ignorance and presumed themselves to have a monopoly on the roles of "teacher" and "specialist." Freire's co-intentionality demands demythologizing the experts' role as the necessary opposite of the students'. Resolution of the student-teacher contradiction does not eliminate need for teachers but points out that teachers must also be students and that students can also be teachers. The notion is hardly new with Freire (one can find it in Aristotle and St. Thomas) and he does not pretend the ideal of dialogical analytic-synthetic education is first seen in his writings. He acknowledges his indebtedness to John Dewey and to existential philosophers like Karl Jaspers who value dialogue, and even dismisses others' concern with his lack of originality by quoting from *Democracy and Education:* "Furthermore, with respect to originality we

always think with Dewey, for whom 'originality is not found in the fantastic, but in the new use of things already known."[57]

Then what does a teacher do? Freire says a teacher is an "inductive presence" in a group of inquirers who leads to the synthesis: educator-educatee, and educatee-educator.[58] The teacher is a subject seeking to know with other subjects. He presents cognitive material for consideration, then reconsiders his earlier presentation in light of students' considerations (reduction, codification, decodification).[59] The teacher is aware that dialogue is not a technique, that it does not start in the classroom, and so prepares a program which recognizes the role students play in the re-creation of knowledge. This role will also involve students in the preparation of their own further education.[60] Teachers can suggest but not predetermine the generative themes which serve to organize the content of dialogue. Not only is unilateral imposition of themes blind to the need for each class to be an encounter among subjects, it is anti-scientific and constitutes cultural invasion.[61]

Expert knowledge is integral to education through conscientization. Men live in history and benefit from praxis and technology developed in former generations. When Freire organized his teams of investigators in the literacy programs, team members were sociologists, psychologists, anthropologists, historians, educators, philosophers, linguists, political scientists, and artists. In the agrarian reforms Freire worked with agronomists whose training was specialized in the areas of soil conservation, crop rotation, animal husbandry, etc., in addition to teams of similar composition to those who worked with him in Brazil. Each person made indispensable, unique contributions because of his or her area of expertise. Their work, however, was aimed at the ultimate objective of raising peasant consciousness to seek humanizing change through problematization of reality. According to Freire all education should utilize expert knowledge, but it should be careful to avoid banking methods and their oppressive consequences. Professionals who try to impose finalities or transfer skills with no intent of humanizing themselves and those with whom they work fail to educate.

    6. *Cultural synthesis is the alternative to cultural invasion.* Freire sets before educators the choice between two opposing theories of cultural action: (1) cultural action for freedom or (2) cultural action for domestication. The closing chapter of *Pedagogy of the Oppressed* argues that education to maintain the status quo or to subvert a revolution is characterized by the oppressors' methodology: the tactics of conquest, division and rule of the people, manipulation, and cultural invasion. Liberating education should discover these tactics as it investigates the shape of people's thinking and realize that as themes they suggest the dialectical opposites of the oppressors' intentions, both as themes and as tactics to be incorporated in cultural action for freedom. Rather than conquest and division, dialogue seeks cooperation and unity. In place of manipulation of the masses, organization is a tactic leading to liberation. More importantly, cultural invasion that attempts to impose foreign or otherwise alienating cultural patterns and beliefs (including the values and myths of an oppressor country or class) suggests the liberating educational possibility of cultural synthesis. In my view the tactic of cultural synthesis is really a synonym for Freire's pedagogy. It is both end and means, since cultural synthesis is another term for praxis. He points out

that cultural synthesis is not a terminal phase of education, but should be present as finality and means at every stage of the educative process.[62]

7. *Careful attention to philosophy of education is not a pedagogical luxury.* Freire has made a timely and important contribution to the field of educational philosophy by his insistence upon the need for authentic praxis. It is impossible to reduce his thought to a collection of other men's ideas both because of his innovative methodology and because of the three accents in his philosophy upon (1) oppression, (2) continued dependence of former colonies upon economic and political decisions of director societies, and (3) the marginalized peoples who constitute the cultures of silence. Americans are familiar with educators like George Counts, John Dewey, Theodore Brameld and scores of others who stressed the anthropological concept of culture and developed the social implications of education, but more often than not those men spoke to an audience which rarely conceived the magnitude of educational work that lies ahead of all the nations on this planet. Freire joins them with a directness and immediacy that can only come from his third world perspective and experience. His extension of the definition of the third world to a non-geographical political concept which includes struggling minorities in first world countries (and for that matter, emergent student consciousness everywhere) places him in the vanguard of contemporary humanistic educational theorists. And the fact that he practices what he preaches not only makes him credible, it compensates for his excesses by way of too easily dividing the entire human race into oppressors and the oppressed.

To those who sneer that Latin American intellectuals have been preoccupied with theoretical concerns at the expense of concrete action for liberation, Freire replies that theory is not opposed to praxis (reflection combined with action), but to *verbalism* (words and thought without action) and to *activism* (naive cultural action devoid of critical consciousness).[63] To those who claim that involving oneself and one's students in an "archaeology of the consciousness" is a waste of time in the face of the urgent social and educational needs of the third world, Freire remarks that wholesale importation and transfer of first world technology and science by educational methods that ignore the consciousness of marginal populations can be as dehumanizing and oppressive as the regimes which suppress people by other methods.[64] To those who assert that modern men and women need less technology and more humanism, Freire says they present a false dilemma, a dilemma resulting from lack of vision of the cultural totality. The choice is not for humanism and against technology, as they are not mutually exclusive. Technology and science are themselves products of culture and can be used either for humanization or alienation. Men need technology, but not dehumanizing technology. To assume that technology and science are neutral overlooks their potentiality for alienation and is as pernicious an error as that made by false humanists who deem science and technology enemies of the race.[65]

The urgent need of millions of people for development can lead them to attempt change of the social structure simply by change of government. But political literacy is not obtained by replacing a vertical political structure and pretending the horizontal structure of man-world relationships does not exist. The two structures overlap and are inseparable from history and culture.[66] If educators act arrogantly and peasants, for example, resort to magical or naive ways of behaving, the educators blame the peasants for being "ungrateful" or "incapable of learning," thus making an error as egregious as the peasants' attribution of crop failure to the will of God or a patron saint's vengeance. Freire says that while peasants who blame disaster upon magic are intransitive, educators who blame peasants for inability to receive deposits of technological information act naively in assuming they can use banking methods to teach.[67] While the examples Freire gives about application of philosophical theory to pedagogy are almost exclusively directed to the prerequisites of literacy and agrarian reform programs, he insists that the same concern for philosophy should permeate all education.

VI

I have no doubt many critics of Paulo Freire will continue to dismiss him as one who offers a "merely political view" of education. Others will admire him for his genius and ability to adapt to the needs and interests of adult illiterates, but will stop short by relegating applicability of his thought to the field of adult education. I would hope the wider implications of his philosophy for all of education—especially realization of the non-neutrality of education and the importance Freire attributes to the roles of student and teacher consciousness—might be examined in greater depth by all who teach, whether in schools, homes, pulpits, or through the media. The sufferings of third world peoples within and beyond our borders are years away from any easy solutions, but they will remain light years away from any serious human effort if educators fail to pose them as problems that demand (but do not defy) resolution.

As I write these words of conclusion to an admittedly deficient study of the life and work of Paulo Freire, Dom Helder Camara of Brazil and Mother Teresa of Calcutta are reminding the Forty-First International Eucharistic Congress in Philadelphia that to spurn the oppressed is to spurn God Himself. It is an affront to human dignity that so many millions must struggle just to survive. Freire has eloquently reminded us that every person must struggle to become human, to divest oneself either of oppressor consciousness or the conviction that the world must remain as we discover it. He is a man of hope who calls us all to the hard work of authentic compassion. May he continue to say "his word."

NOTES

1. Female readers of Freire frequently call attention to his discussion of human beings in an apparently chauvinistic manner by use of *man* or *men* to speak of the human race. He has acknowledged this as an oversight, and I believe publication of two booklets *Liberation of Woman: To Change the World and Re-Invent Life* (1974) and *Toward a Woman's World* (1975) by Freire's Geneva *Institut d'Action Culturelle*, plus the use of the non-sexist pronoun *s/he* in Seabury Press' translation of two of his works are ample evidence of his concern to include women in every phase of human liberation. For my part, wherever I have conformed to contemporary English usage in this book and used *man* or *men*, I understand him to speak of all humans, male and female of every age.

2. Paulo Freire, *Cultural Action for Freedom* (Cambridge: *Harvard Educational Review* and Center for the Study of Development and Social Change, 1970), p. 12.

3. Paulo Freire, *Pedagogy of the Oppressed* (New York: Herder and Herder, 1970), p. 91.

4. Paulo Freire, "Acción Cultural y Reforma Agraria," *Sobre la Acción Cultural* (México, D.F.: Secretariado Social Mexicano, 1970), p. 105. (Translation from the Spanish text is by this writer.)

5. Freire, *Pedagogy of the Oppressed*, p. 91.

6. *Ibid.*, p. 92. (Emphasis is Freire's.)

7. Idealization of the political superstructure by myths is one of the themes Freire developed regarding Brazilian society in *Education as the Practice of Freedom*. Elsewhere Freire refers to the relationship of permanence and change in the social structure in *Cultural Action for Freedom*, p. 33, and also in *Pedagogy of the Oppressed*, pp. 72, 180.

8. Freire, *Cultural Action for Freedom*, pp. 13-16. Cf. also Paulo Freire, "Los Campesinos También Pueden Ser Autores de sus Propios Textos de Lectura," *Sobre la Acción Cultural*, pp. 40-41.

9. Paulo Freire, *Conscientisation and Liberation* (Geneva: *Institute d'Action Culturelle*, 1972), p. 5.

10. Freire, *Pedagogy of the Oppressed*, p. 69.

11. Paulo Freire, Preface to *Pedagogy of the Oppressed*, p. 22f.

12. Freire, *Cultural Action for Freedom*, p. 36.

13. Robert Sokolowski, "Edmund Husserl and the Principles of Phenomenology," *Twentieth Century Thinkers*, ed. by John Ryan (New York: Alba House, 1967), p. 138f.

14. Freire, *Pedagogy of the Oppressed*, p. 70.

15. Paulo Freire, "The Political Literacy Process—an Introduction" (unpublished manuscript translation of an article prepared for publication in the *Lutherische Monatshefte*, Hannover, Germany, Oct. 1970), p. 1.

16. Freire, *Pedagogy of the Oppressed*, p. 27.

17. *Ibid.*, pp. 36-37.

18. Paulo Freire, "Conscientizar para Liberar," *Contacto*, VIII, No. 1 (Feb., 1971), p. 43.

19. Freire, *Cultural Action for Freedom*, p. 30.

92   PAULO FREIRE

20. Freire, "Conscientizar para Liberar," p. 44.

21. *Ibid.*, p. 47.

22. Freire, "The Political Literacy Process—an Introduction," p. 11.

23. Freire, *Pedagogy of the Oppressed*, p. 175.

24. Freire, "Conscientizar para Liberar," pp. 50-51.

25. Paulo Freire, "Education for Awareness: A Talk with Paulo Freire," *Risk*, VI, No. 4 (April, 1970), p. 11.

26. Paulo Freire, "Investigación de la Temática Generadora," *Sobre la Acción Cultural,* p. 75. (Translation by the present writer.)

27. Paulo Freire, "El Rol del Trabajador Social en el Proceso de Cambio," *Sobre la Acción Cultural*, pp. 121-124.

28. Some interpreters of Freire seem to imply that conscientization is the supreme value in Freire's philosophy. In an interview Freire granted me in Seattle in January, 1973, he said this is a misunderstanding of his philosophy and an erroneous interpretation of the role he claims for consciousness in changing social structures. Misinterpretations of his emphasis upon conscientization often cause him to be accused of idealism. Emergence of consciousness through conscientization is an indispensable condition of authentic praxis and hence an important human value, but Freire says it is only a means to the higher end of permanent transformation of society. For this reason I prefer in these pages to use Brameld's term "value-means" to speak of conscientization and the other means to achieve Freireian praxis.

29. Freire, *Pedagogy of the Oppressed*, pp. 65, 120-121.

30. Paulo Freire, "The Educational Role of the Churches in Latin America," *Pasos*, No. 9 (Oct., 1972). Translated in edited form in Latin American Documentation Series of the U.S. Catholic Conference (LADOC), III, No. 14 (Dec. 1972), p. 9.

31. Freire, *Cultural Action for Freedom*, p. 18.

32. Paulo Freire, *La Educación como Práctica de la Libertad* (México, D.F.: Siglo Veintiuno Editores, S.A., 1971), pp. 41-43.

33. Freire, *Pedagogy of the Oppressed*, pp. 169-170.

34. *Ibid.*, pp. 179-180.

35. Freire, *Cultural Action for Freedom*, p. 47.

36. Paulo Freire, "El Compromiso del Professional con la Sociedad," *Sobre la Acción Cultural*, pp. 150-151. (Translation by the present writer.)

37. Freire, *Cultural Action for Freedom*, pp. 51-52.

38. Paulo Freire, "Carta a un Joven Teólogo," *Contacto*, IX, No. 1 (Feb., 1972), p. 65.

39. *Ibid.*

40. Freire, *Cultural Action for Freedom*, p. 60.

41. Freire, "The Educational Role of the Churches in Latin America," pp. 1-4.

42. *Ibid.*, pp. 5-14.

43. Freire, "Carta a un Joven Teólogo," p. 66. (Translation is by the present writer.)

44. Freire, "The Political Literacy Process—an Introduction," p. 8.

45. The two best recent expositions of Freire's literacy methods I have seen are Harriet Sherwin's "Paulo Freire, His Philosophy and Pedagogy of Teaching Reading," (unpublished monograph delivered at the Sixth World Congress on Reading in Singapore, Aug. 19, 1976), and Cynthia Brown's "Literacy in 30 Hours: Paulo Freire's Process in Northeast Brazil," *Social Policy* (July-August, 1974), pp. 25-32.

46. Paulo Freire, "Los Campesinos También Pueden Ser Autores de sus Propios Textos de Lectura," p. 46.

47. Freire, *Cultural Action for Freedom*, p. 31.

48. Paulo Freire, *¿Extensión o Communicación?* (Cuernavaca: CIDOC Cuaderno No. 25, 1968), p. 14/90.

49. Freire, *Pedagogy of the Oppressed*, pp. 53-56.

50. *Ibid.*, pp. 58-61.

51. Freire, "Investigación de la Temática Generadora," *Sobre la Acción Cultural*, p. 54.

52. Freire, *Pedagogy of the Oppressed*, p. 59.

53. Paulo Freire, "La Práctica del Método Psicosocial," *Sobre la Acción Cultural*, p. 40.

54. Freire, "Education for Awareness," p. 8.

55. Freire, "The Political Literacy Process—an Introduction," p. 10.

56. Freire, *Conscientisation and Liberation*, pp. 8-10.

57. Freire, *La Educación como Práctica de la Libertad*, p. 121. (Translation is by this writer.)

58. Freire. "The Political Literacy Process—an Introduction," p. 8.

59. Freire, *Pedagogy of the Oppressed*, pp. 68-69.

60. Freire, "Investigación de la Temática Generadora," *Sobre la Acción Cultural*, pp. 65-66.

61. Freire, *¿Extensión o Communicación?*, pp. 14/93-94.

62. Freire, *Pedagogy of the Oppressed*, pp. 182-183.

63. Freire, "La Práctica del Método Psísocial," *Sobre la Acción Cultural*, pp. 33-34.

64. Freire, *Cultural Action for Freedom*, p. 47.

65. Freire, "El Compromiso del Profesional con la Sociedad," *Sobre la Acción Cultural*, pp. 150-151.

66. Freire, *¿Extensión o Communicación?*, pp. 14/63-66.

67. Freire, "El Compromiso del Profesional con la Sociedad," *Sobre la Acción Cultural*, p. 150.